Tales Of 47

This book is dedicated to my youngest brother
GUY JOSEPH MARTIN
29 January 1952 – 24 February 2010

Acknowledgements

My first book which was a solo effort about the B.C. Penitentiary was written in about 4-6 hrs over 2 days, whereas this one I have worked on for at least 2 years, and owe thanks to many people.

First my daughters. Wendy Martin-Stroyan who has helped this computer illiterate body with a great deal of computer work. Penny Martin who has "pestered" me continually to get the thing finished, and also persuaded Wendy to help with the computer stuff. My granddaughter Jailena, who installed many of the photos ('cause I didn't know how); and my niece Angela Dereume and her husband Patrick Keaney who went to a great deal of work in editing this tome. Unfortunately some of their work was not included....again because of my lack of computer knowledge and inability to switch from a Mac to a PC and back again. If they changed anything in Joe's diary it has not been acted upon, because I felt that his diary should be printed "as is" largely because it shows the trip of a lifetime in the eyes of a 12 year old boy. I have however added photos to Joe's diary, because I had them and was there at the time.

Also of course, a debt of thanks to my siblings who submitted stories; several of the same tales are sent by people who perhaps saw the same incident a little differently. In some cases I had yet another view, BUT I have related their memory. One of my siblings had a different version of a story of mine, but the printed version is how I remembered it, thus my version is represented here.

If there are any mistakes, then they must be mine. Also I should mention that I have included the "cast" of this performance for the benefit of non-Martins so they have an idea of whereabouts in the family order they appear.

A.E. Martin November 2018

NAME	WHERE BORN	DATE	
Francis Martin (Father)	Born 39 Adelphi Street, Salford	15th May 1906	5 JUNE 1978
Mary (Nee Mather) Martin (Mother)	Born 92 Broughton Road, Salford,	7th April 1907	26 JUNE 199
Mary Frances Martin	Born, 43 Silk Street, Salford	22nd June 1929	
Francis Gerard Martin	Born 43 Silk Street, Salford	16th October 1930	21 DEC 201
Teresa Martin	Born 43 Silk Street, Salford	29th June 1932	
	Died 43 Silk Street, Salford	29th June 1932	
Anthony Edmund Martin	Born 15 Walsall Street, Salford	24th September 1933	
Thomas Edmund Martin	Born 15 Walsall Street, Salford	26th June 1935	19 SEP 19
George Neville Martin	Born 15 Walsall Street, Salford	2nd April 1937	11 FEB 201
Margaret Bernadette Martin	Born 15 Walsall Street, Salford	6th January 1939	20 NOV 20
James Patrick Martin	Born 15 Walsall, Street, Salford	14th July 1942	
Pauline Ann Martin	Born 47 Broughton Road, Salford	9th March 1944	
Gregory John Martin	Born 47 Broughton Road, Salford	5th July 1946	
Peter Damien Martin	Born 47 Broughton road, Salford	12th June 1948	
Angela Mary Martin	Born 47 Broughton Road, Salford	28th May 1950	
Guy Joseph Martin	Born 47 Broughton Road, Salford	29th January 1952	24 FEB 201

Table of Contents

Acknowledgements. v
Foreword 1
Frank Martin 3
My Mam. 10
Interruption!. 45
Reminiscenses 51
    That Man 54
    The Boys' Bedroom 56
    The Wireless 57
    Joe 59
    Gerard 63
    Tom 64
    Neville 65
    Pauline 69
    John. 71
    Mary 76
    Margaret 79
    James 79
    Part II of the Epistle according to James 90
    My Working Life. 94
    Education. 97
    J & F Brookes. 98
    Belle Vue 99
    Beswick Primary School 102
    Martin Brothers 103
    Nazareth House. 105
    Carmelite Convent 106
    Clifford Turner 110

    The Hollies Convent Grammar School......... 112
    Shay Lane 117
    Mode Wheel Abattoir 118
    The Rag Trade 119
    Littleton Road Flats........................ 120
    Bruntwood Estates 122
    Adsega 123
    Bayer Dyestuffs 124
    All Saints Primary School Mosses Gate 125
    Tootal Broadhurst Lee 125
    Memories of 47 126
    Harry Marshall............................. 135
Locked Out!..................................... 143
Travel 151
National Service 153
Ted Mather 161
A Surprise Trip to Canada from
Salford Docks in 1965............................ 163

Appendix...................................... 225

Tales Of 47

Including GJ Martin trip diary

Anthony E. Martin

Foreword

The idea for this book originated with my brother Joe, and sometime after his untimely death I decided that I would try to complete it. However some explanation is required, in that although I am compiling these stories, I should NOT be considered the author, but rather the Narrator, as the stories belong to my siblings, many of whom submitted comments. In some cases I received the same stories from different people, often told from a different viewpoint. Also, of course, the people telling them were of different ages, and therefore saw things in a different light. In addition some saw things that others didn't, and so even though it means some duplication I will give the stories exactly as they were given to me. I will try, mostly to tell these tales in the order in which they occurred, but there are a couple more things to be said before the stories start. There were two areas which affected our lives at "47"; One being St Sebastian's RC Church, which was a large part of our lives. Besides being our parish church, it was also a Dominican Priory for which we had a great affinity. It will certainly be mentioned throughout the book. The other was our next-door neighbour Harry Marshall who lived at 49 Broughton Road. He too will be mentioned in many of the stories. So now we can get down to the "Nitty Gritty".

*To appreciate these tales,
you will need to know something of the couple
who bred and raised this tribe!*

First my Dad

Frank Martin

My Dad was born on 15 May 1906 at 39 Adelphi St in the shadow of St John's Cathedral, Salford, the ninth of twelve children. His father died when he was about 6 and so he knew very little about him. His mother subsequently married a man called Tommy Purcell who was not a good man (and brought 2 of his children into the family). Frank went to school until he was about 13, but while he was at school he started working for a greengrocer(Mr Wright) and saved some of the money he earned – for safekeeping & to prevent it being used for booze for his stepfather he tied it in his shirt-tail when he went to bed. Eventually he had enough to buy a suit, which he was only able to wear once before it went to "Uncles". When my Mam told me this I wondered what "Uncles" was but eventually found out it was the pawnbrokers (and yes it was Tommy Purcell that took it there for beer-money!) Eventually my Dad became a fitter for Hamilton & Sons in Ancoats and stayed there for FIFTY-FOUR years! My Dad had a hard life, he got married in 1928, and was able to rent their first house in Silk St; a one up, one down, with a water pipe that was shared with 4 – 5 other families, and an outside loo (also shared). When he rented the house, he also bought some furniture from the man who rented it before. I know there was at least a table & 4 chairs, and possibly a bed & other items.. So having lived through the First World War he was now entering married life at the beginning of the Depression. Of course, throughout the narrative my Dad is mentioned rather frequently.

Vol. I. No. 14   Christmas 1953

THE
CATHOLIC MOTHER

A BETTER CRIB   CHRISTMAS STORIES

FESTIVE FEATURES   THE DOCTOR'S ADVICE

FICTION • HOMECRAFT • FEATURES • FASHIONS

PRICE THREEPENCE

Household Forum

HELD BY THE SALFORD DIOCESE

CHRISTMAS CRACKERS

Small Boy (watching Mother serve the Christmas Pudding)—"Is that big piece of pudding for Baby?"
Mother—"No, for you, dear."
Small Boy—"What! THAT tiny bit?"

* * *

First Small Boy—"We've got an electric train and I've got a wireless, and we've got an airgun, and. . . ."
Second Small Boy—"And I'll tell you what else you've got!"
First Small Boy—"What?"
Second Small Boy—"Swank!"

* * *

Little Willie (sobbing for freedom)—"But, Mummy, I don't want to carry two bags for you! I wish I was grown-up like Father!"
Mother (firmly)—"If you want to be like your Father, you'll do as I tell you."

* * *

COOKERY CORNER

Many of the Lancashire towns that come into the Salford Diocese are famous for their special recipes. Look up Bury Pudding or Eccles Cakes in any cookery book. But perhaps two of the most famous deserve a mention here.

Lancashire Hot-Pot

This makes a delicious supper for a cold night.

Ingredients:

Some neck of Mutton.	Flour.
2 lbs. Potatoes.	Salt and Pepper.
1 Onion.	half-pint cold water.
2 ozs. Mushrooms (if liked).	

Cut the meat into chops, cutting off some of the fat. (Stewing steak can be used, cut into small pieces.) Sprinkle with flour, salt and pepper. Lay on the bottom of a fire-proof dish, cover with chopped onion and mushrooms, then add potatoes cut into fairly small pieces, add more salt and pepper and the cold water. Cook uncovered in a slow oven (regulo 4) for about two hours.

Prestwich Tart. A favourite with children of all ages.

Directions:

Line a plate with short crust pastry; place on it about 2 ozs. of chopped stoned dates. Add three tablespoons-full of slightly warmed, black treacle.

Cover with layer of pastry, trim edges and cook in a hot oven for about 20-25 minutes.

MAKE CHRISTMAS-TIME SAFETY-TIME!

NEVER leave a small child, even for a few minutes, in a room with a fire, without first seeing the fireguard is in place. Children will reach up to the mantelpiece to get something they want.

IF you have to put an infant down, to fetch something or to answer the phone or door in a hurry (if the cot or pram isn't handy), the *floor*, on a rug, towel, or shawl is the safest place. The infant cannot fall any further!

WHEN removing a safety pin from baby's nappy, make a habit of closing it. Then, if it gets mislaid, the panic is not so great.

* * *

TIMELY TIPS

THE moment you empty a carton, packet, tin, or bottle, when cooking, throw the lid, top or stopper into your shopping bag. This will save a lot of time when you try to remember what you are short of in making out your shopping list.

WHEN steel needles rust, a rub with a cinder will soon restore their usefulness.

AFTER boiling milk in an aluminium saucepan, an immediate rub round with a damp cloth prevents fat sediment clinging.

PUT your kettle in the side oven before going to bed at night. You will find that it takes less time to boil in the morning.

A SMEAR of margarine round the rim of a milk pan prevents the milk from boiling over.

WHEN bottle tops are stiff, run the bottles under a hot tap. This will ease the stiffness.

WHEN boiling cauliflower, add a teaspoon of milk. It will keep the cauliflower white.

* * *

WE ARE PROUD OF

Mrs. Martin, of Pendleton, mother of eight sons and four daughters, ranging in age from 24 years to 17 months old, with the following lovely Catholic names: Mary, Gerard, Anthony, Edmund, George, Margaret, James, Pauline, John, Peter, Angela and Joseph. Mary is at present with relations in Canada, Gerard has been in the Navy, Anthony is in the Army and Edmund in the Air Force.

The six older children have all won scholarships to Convents and Colleges. Angela and Joseph are still too young to go to school and Mrs. Martin says what a great help are the

THE CATHOLIC MOTHER

older children with the housework and minding the little ones. In spite of all difficulties, Mrs. Martin has never gone out to work and believes definitely " that a mother's place is in the home." She always has the younger ones in to mid-day meals. " How else," she says, " can you train them in good manners?" She is blessed with a very good husband and the accompanying photograph shows how lovely and happy they all are.

We also acclaim our beloved National President, Mrs. Gervase Kemhall, one-time Mayor of Eccles, a Justice of the Peace, and a County Councillor.

And Mrs. Hugh Lee, Past National President, one-time Lady Mayoress of Manchester, mother of eight children, and proud grandmother of twenty-two grandchildren.

THE MARTIN FAMILY

LANCASHIRE GLORY

The Diocese of Salford comes in the County of Lancashire, which is famous for many Martyrs in penal times. One of the best known is **Blessed Ambrose Barlow**, who was born near Manchester, at Barlow Hall, on the banks of the Mersey, in 1585. One of fourteen children, he was christened Edward, in the Parish Church of Didsbury. According to the custom of that time, he was sent, as a boy of twelve, to be a page in the home of a nobleman who, unfortunately, was not a Catholic. Edward strayed from his faith for a time, but on being reconciled, went to Douay to train for the priesthood under Cardinal Allen. He then joined the revived order of St. Benedict and was ordained a priest in 1617.

As Dom Ambrose, he immediately returned to England and spent twenty-four years ministering in and about his own countryside. He was arrested on April 25th, 1641, having just finished saying Mass, and was imprisoned in Lancaster Jail.

After being tried for his faith, he was hanged and his members disembowelled and cast into boiling oil. We are proud to state that his skull is preserved in a niche on the stairway of Wardley Hall, the residence of the Bishop of Salford.

Another Martyr from our Diocese, **Blessed John Southworth**, of Samlesbury, was hanged at Tyburn and his shrine is in the Church of St. Mary (founded 1690), Samlesbury, between Preston and Blackburn. It is said that while a prisoner in Lancaster Jail, Blessed John gave a last absolution to Fr. Edmund Arrowsmith, when the latter was on his way to martyrdom.

HAPPIER— by the dozen

HAPPY FAMILIES

TAKE a tip from cheery Mrs. Mary Martin. "Here's the secret to a full and happy life," she says. "Children—and lots of 'em!"

And 47-year-old Mrs. Martin, of Broughton Road, Salford, ought to know. She has twelve, ranging from a 25-year-old daughter to a son aged two.

Like Topsy, the Martin family "just growed." "We didn't set out to have a large family but I wouldn't have missed the experience for anything," she said at her home. "I'm not sure whether it is cheaper by the dozen, but it's certainly happier!"

Two of the children, Mary (25) and Tom (19), are away now—Mary in Canada and Tom in the R.A.F. But feeding and clothing the others is still a problem.

MEALS—staggered

They all sit down together for the main evening meal. Other meals are "staggered."

At least 10lbs. of potatoes go into one meal. The baker delivers over 35 loaves a week and the milkman leaves 56 bottles of milk in a week.

Clothes? "I've always made most of the clothes myself," said Mrs. Martin. "Now, Margaret (15) gives me a hand with the sewing and knitting. All the other children are allocated jobs about the house.

"I have only recently acquired a washing machine. Previously I did the family wash in the cellar. It took me three days to do the family wash."

Still at school are Margaret James (12), Pauline (10), John (8), Peter (6), and Angela (4). Gerard (23), Anthony (21), and George (17) are out at work augmenting the family income.

In addition Mrs. Martin gets £2 8s. family allowance. Her husband Frank is an engineer. He earns about £7 a week.

Baby of the family is two-year-old Joseph. Six of the children won scholarships to grammar schools and technical colleges.

HOLIDAYS—in turn

The Martins started married life in a one-up one-down house in Silk-street, Salford. Later they moved to Walsall-street, but that house soon became too small and they moved to their present home.

Holidays? The last one they had together was at Formby in 1939. Balancing the family budget for so many people is no easy job and the Martins can't always afford a holiday "en bloc." So now they take it in turns.

Mrs. Martin left school at 13 and before she was married looked after her invalid mother. "The home has always been my life," she said.

And as for Mr. Martin—"Children don't worry me. I was one of fourteen myself!"

TALES OF FORTY-SEVEN

from the Manchester Evening News

(note – Anthony submitted a story on his family with the goal of earning 10 shillings and sixpence...the paper came and interviewed their Mam and Anthony still collected the 10/6d

Happier – by the Dozen

Take a tip from cheery Mrs. Mary Martin. "Here's the secret to a full and happy life" She says "children and lots of them".

47 year old Mrs. Martin of Broughton road Salford, ought to know. She has 12 ranging from a 25 year old daughter to a son aged 2.

Like "Topsy", the Martin family just "growed". "We didn't set out to have a large family but I wouldn't have missed the experience for anything," she said at her home. "I'm not sure whether it is cheaper by the dozen but it is certainly happier."

Two of the children, Mary 25 and Tom 19 are away now. Mary in Canada and Tom in the RAF but feeding and clothing the others is still a problem.

MEALS – STAGGERED

They all sit down together for the main evening meal but other meals are staggered.

At least 10 pounds of potatoes go into one meal, the baker delivers over 35 loaves a week and the milkman leaves 56 bottles of milk in a week.

Clothes? "I've always made most of the clothes myself" said Mrs. Martin. "Now, Margaret (15) gives me a hand with the sewing and knitting". All the other children are allocated jobs about the house.

"I have only recently acquired a washing machine. Previously I did it in the cellar, it took me three days to do the family wash".

Still at school, our Margaret, James (12) Pauline (10), John (8), Peter (6) and Angela (4). Gerard (23), Anthony (21) and Neville (17) are out at work augmenting the family income.

In addition, Mrs. Martin gets 2 Pounds 8 shillings family allowance. Her husband Frank is an engineer, he earns about 7 pound a week

Baby of the family is 2 year old Joseph. Six of the children won scholarships to grammar schools and technical colleges.

HOLIDAYS – IN TURN

The Martins started married life in a one-up one-down house in Silk Street, Salford. Later they moved to Walsall street but that house soon became too small and they moved to their present home.

Holidays ? The last one they had together was at Formby in 1939. Balancing the family budget for so many people is no easy job and the Martins can't always afford a holiday "on block" so now they take it in turns.

Mrs. Martin left school at 13 and before she was married looked after her invalid Mother. "The home has always been my life" she said.

And as for Mr. Martin – children don't worry me, I was one of 14 myself.

My Mam

My Mam (the most revered and loved woman that I have ever known) was born at 92 Broughton Rd (next door to the Bijou cinema) on 7 April 1907, the eldest of 8 children. Her mother (Mary Emma Mather nee Walton) was quite deaf as a result of working in a cotton mill where she ran 4 looms. She was also asthmatic and as a result my Mam spent a lot of time looking after her siblings and had to do washing & ironing – and this was when there were no washing machines, flat irons were heated up in the fire and clothes were dried by putting them through a mangle which had to be turned by hand – back-breaking work. As a result of all this, her health suffered, and finally the doctor said that she needed to have a rest, so, at the age of 16 she was sent to Canada to her Uncle George where she remained for two years. A couple more snippets about my Mam: she did not have much formal education but was non the less wise and smart. One time I must have been a little bossy (unusually!), don't remember what I'd said, or to whom, but I do recall her response which was, "You're not a Corporal here you know!" I'd just finished my national service. Another time just after having her ninth baby (our John) some woman very pointedly said, "Is this your last?" to which my Mam replied, "No, it's my latest!" One time she was near the wool shop on the corner of Borough St and Whit Lane, and saw some bolts of cloth fall off a lorry (honest she did), they were probably mill-ends. Anyway she picked them up, went into the wool shop, and they called the police who came and picked them up. Many months later the police called and told her to come and collect the cloth as they had not been claimed. I remember my daughters got new dresses out of that! Her Dad, Ted Mather, will get a page of his own but here is what little we know of her Mother. Mary Emma Walton was born on 18 December 1879. Her family ran a dairy in Salford (in my time it was in Union St.). She worked in a mill, and because of the constant noise of the shuttles, like many mill employees, she became deaf; and also like many mill employees she could lip read. Probably her employment caused her asthmatic condition. At some stage she had Alopecia which caused her hair to fall out. A specialist gave her husband a prescription which contained 3 simple ingredients, at which point Ted said "I'm paying you 3 guineas for this???" The reply was, "No! You are paying me for my knowledge/skills!!" She died at the age of 47 in 1927.

So, now I'll start with the actual story! My Mam and Dad were married in St. Sebastian's church on August 8th, 1928 by Father Antoninus McGuire who was at that time the Prior. It was a quiet wedding because the Mather family were still in mourning for the death of Mary Emma.

My Dad had rented a house at 43 Silk St in the Adelphi and that's where they started their married life. When he rented the house, he also bought some furniture from the previous renter, and the first thing he did was to change the locks on the door, and slept there that night. During the night, he heard a noise, went and checked, and there was the former renter with a handcart. My Dad surmised that he had tried to get in (but of course the lock had been changed!) There is a plan of the house at Appendix A. It was a one up, one down, with a shared toilet (shared with 5 other families) and a shared stand pipe in the yard, which is where they had to get whatever water they needed.

It was in this house, that Mary, Gerard, and Theresa were born. This was of course during the depression and obviously they struggled. At one time my Dad was laid off, and one day my Mam went to buy food and offered a sovereign to pay for it. (This was the sovereign that my Dad had given her on their wedding day). The shop keeper, on hearing of its origin told my Mam, she could pay him when she had the money! (Showing that she was very trustworthy even then). The sovereign was eventually given to the first Martin Grandson (Chris Martin). I of course don't know that much about Silk St. but it may be mentioned in some of Mary's contributions. I do know that their Parish church was St John's Cathedral and many years later when My Mam was living in Swinton, her parish priest was a priest from the Cathedral, and they had many mutual friends.

In time, (actually 1933) my Dad was able to rent a new house in what was called the Lobby Field (I don't know why). The house was 15 Walsall St and I was the first baby born on that housing estate. He tried to persuade some of his sisters to move there, but they preferred to stay where they were (Blackfriars).

This was a tremendous improvement for my parents. The house had a kitchen, living room, very small pantry, and a coal hole. Upstairs there were 2 bedrooms, and a bathroom. There was also a garden, back & front! There is also a plan of this house (courtesy of Joe Martin, in the appendix).

I was born there on September 24th 1933, Tom on June 27th 1935, Neville on April 2nd 1937 (of course we always told him how lucky he was not to have been born the day before as he would have been an April Fool!), Margaret on January 6th 1939, and James on July 14th 1942.

(#15 – second house from left)

One of the advantages of living there is that once again we were in St Sebastian's parish, and were close to our Grandad's house. Initially he and his family lived at 32 Milnethorpe St. which at that time was lit by gas, no electricity. I remember that we used to have to go up to Broad Street to get "accumulators" charged for the radio. The accumulators were heavy, made of glass, and were usually put in the trolley to make it easier to carry. Eventually they moved to 1 Littleton Road, across from the Racecourse.

There are lots of memories (for what Angela calls the Big Ones) from Walsall St, which will be told now, but not necessarily in chronological order. In this house cooking was done either at the fireplace, which had an oven or, on a small gas ring in the kitchen which was paid for by putting money in the meter; no money equals no gas. We had our meals in the living room, and one day after tea (which is the 5pm meal), we had gone out to play, when all of a sudden there is a commotion, our Neville was missing. So we searched all over the neighborhood, no Neville! Checked the house again, still no Neville. My Dad was just about ready to go to the the police box, when Neville was found! He had been sitting on an armchair, on the far side of the table, my Dad took off the tea cozy & threw it at Neville and it landed on his head. He was quite small at the time and we presume the heat sent him to sleep, and he sunk below the level of the table and couldn't be seen.

We were living in this house in 1939 when we had our famous holiday at Formby! We (the children) did not at that time know some of the facts that we know now, and which have been discussed on Facebook at the time this is being written. Gerard and I, in our discussions when I stayed with him in England, often wondered how our parents could have afforded to take six children away for a week in a hotel! Wow! So now the story can be told. A philanthropist (whose name I don't know), either bought or leased a hotel called Stella Maris which was right on the beach at Formby. He did this to provide holidays for Catholic working class families in Lancashire. I have to guess that he organized it through the Parishes, because on that holiday everyone was from St Sebastian's Parish, and at least 2 priests were included. We were there at the end of May, beginning of June, and I know we were back for June 10th because that is when Aunty Winnie got married. Several things happened at Formby. We were on the shore one day and saw a submarine, and saw it submerge, it was called HMS Thetis. We found out much later that it was on its first trials, and it never came up. All the crew were drowned. One day while walking to the village, we heard guns firing, and of course much later, realized it was troops preparing for the war.

In my particular case, Formby was to be part of my life on a couple of occasions. I'm guessing that it was probably 1945 when I was about 12, 2 nuns came to the Parish from Patricroft where they operated an orphanage. They wished to sell magazines and collect money for the foreign missions. Well some priest from church took them down to No 1 to see Ted Mather (my Grandad), and of course he came up with a solution – most of his solutions involved me! "Oh yes, Anthony can take you round, he can use the outdoor books to find the addresses", and of course Anthony did! "Outdoor Books"- Books with names and addresses of Parishioners. People used these to go round on a Sunday afternoon to collect funds for church. I suspect it probably took 2 days, just the job a 12 yr old boy wanted to do in his school holidays!!! Well, thats fine, I got it done, but some time later, I was invited to go on a holiday with the orphans (Surely I was the most unlikely orphan)....where to...Yes Formby! Well whilst I was there, I went exploring with some other lads, and we found a real neat place! There were ropes tied to trees where you could swing, just like Tarzan, walls just made for climbing, places to tunnel under. It just couldn't have been better for a 12 year old boy!

Mind you I didn't have the same impression when I was in the Army in 1951 and went to the same place. It was of course an Assault Course, and I was going over it at 2am in February when it was bitterly cold! What is even stranger, we were training to go to the jungles of Malaya, you know where it is hot & humid, didn't make a lot of sense to swing across a stream, fall off the rope and break the ice in the stream; I didn't think there was any ice in Malaya, except at Raffles Hotel!

We were living in Walsall St. when war was declared – September 3rd 1939, but even before that I remember us being in the back bedroom, watching the searchlights practising, with planes flying around, trying to catch the planes in their beams, and before that, during daylight, we watched all the barrage balloons being raised. To us there seemed to be hundreds of them, and we certainly couldn't count them. For those who are too young to know, the purpose of the balloons, was, hopefully, to make enemy planes hit the cables and crash.

The day after war was declared, we were all evacuated, except for my Dad. Mary went to Accrington, Gerard to Rawtenstall, Anthony and Tom to Waterfoot, Neville, Margaret and my Mam to Waterfoot. Margaret was a baby (9 months old), Neville was about 2 and he was in the house next door to where Mam and Margaret were. I was not too badly off, and was in a house close to a farm. Tom had an absolutely awful billet where the people were cruel and unkind.

When we arrived in Waterfoot, I remember being in a church hall and women walking around, looking at us, and saying – I'll take that one – maybe not quite the same as a slave market but bad enough.

This only lasted about 3 months, and I believe our parents decided if we are going to suffer we'll all suffer together and so we all came home. Mind you the war was still on, and so there was loads of fun for little boys, probably not for my Mam and Dad. At some time the government issued Anderson shelters to those people who had gardens, and that included us. So, my Dad dug a hole, erected the shelter, then covered most of it with dirt. I think it was 6ft x 8ft, made of corrugated steel, and in our case had a pipe sticking out of the ground to ensure we had fresh air if it got completely buried. Eventually my Dad made 3 bunk beds on one side in which we slept head to toe, and one on the floor. He eventually installed electric light, and almost electrocuted himself in the process.

For us boys, after every raid, we couldn't wait to get out and collect shrapnel, bits of bombs and bullets, and in some cases unexploded incendiary bombs! One night there was a particularly heavy thump which shook the shelter, so I was quickly out after the all clear sounded, hoping to find an incendiary bomb, however all it was, was a piece of shrapnel about 4" square, and 3/4 " thick. There was many a house with a couple of bombs on the mantelpiece as ornaments! (but not ours). One day Gerard and me found a couple of bullets, we took them home, put the bullet in the vice, and knocked the casing off. This gave us access to the cordite inside, which we then made a trail of it in the garden, and the set fire to it! For us, it was like Cowboys in the movies blowing up the entrance to a mine! One day my uncle James found a large shell on the road outside their house. He picked it up, took it to the police box on the corner and said, 'ere what do I do with this then?" But all the copper could say was, "Don't give it to me!" They finished up putting it in a bucket of water to await arrival of the bomb disposal squad.

Another time, a bomb fell very close to my Grandad's house. There was a fair bit of shrapnel in the house, and about 7 pieces in a wall, all around a statue, but the statue never got broken (the windows did!) The bomb was a direct hit on 2 messenger boys, and I recall seeing my Uncle Billy Molloy scraping up their remains, however he missed a piece, which had landed in the garden at No 1. My Auntie Kath, found it and said hey someones been looting the butchers. However, my Mam knew what it was, and our Mary had a little wooden box which had been made by Batty or Frank Gaughran. Mam says give me that box, and she buried that bit of flesh in the garden. That day people kept calling at No 1, asking if Joe Mather was home, he was also a messenger boy. Nobody knew who the two boys were that had been killed. Eventually Joe came home, he had fallen asleep in an air raid shelter! Big relief to lots of people. It turned out that one of the boys was Sidney Lomax (one of the boys in the Formby pictures).

One night, we were all at home, except Mary who was in a house down the street, keeping another girl company because the girl's mother was at our house. Well, the wireless was on, women talking, children playing, so it was quite noisy. Blackout regulations were in effect, all the windows were covered and my Dad had rigged up a device. He attached a cylinder on a string above the light bulb, and with one end attached to the door. When the door opened, the cylinder descended over the light bulb so that no light could be seen outside. This particular night, every now and again there would be a tremendous hammering on the back door, but when the door was opened there was no-one there! We all figured it was someone playing robbers knock and eventually ignored it until all of a sudden the door opened and there was our Mary. During all the noise, the air raid sirens had gone and we hadn't heard them. Mary and this other girl were alone in the house, and naturally were quite frightened. So they CRAWLED down the back lane, because they could see enemy planes and were afraid the planes could see them and would machine gun them. They went into our shelter, and kept dashing out and hammering on the door and dashing back to the shelter before anyone answered it. They only came out when the "All Clear" sounded, and we didn't hear that in the house either.

The people in the house on the other side of our back lane, (which was actually called Oswald St.) for some reason did not have shelters, so when the bombing started, one lady, Mrs Billings asked if she could come in our shelter. Well of course she could. The first night she came on her own, and said that her husband had said, "I'm not getting out of bed for Hitler!" The next night he did come to the shelter, because a bomb had dropped nearby, and BLEW him out of bed! Eventually, those people went and sheltered in the crypt of St Georges church at the end of the street, and subsequently a shelter was built on a piece of waste ground, where the anti-aircraft guns had been. Some of those people had just come out for fresh air when a Land Mine, a very big bomb attached to a parachute, dropped. The explosion blew them back into the crypt, but no-one was seriously injured.

My Grandad had somewhat the same attitude. He had no shelter, and was advised to go down the cellar during air-raids. "What! Me go down the cellar because of Hitler..No Way!" So instead, he sat in front of the fireplace, where there was probably still a few cinders burning. When the bomb dropped nearby, somebody had gone in to check up on him. He was still sitting in his armchair, covered in soot, with little white circles round his eyes, and blowing soot off his moustache!

At Christmas time 1940 Salford had its big blitz. When we came out of the shelter in the morning, the sky was red, just like a forest fire, except it was the docks that were burning. The next door neighbour said to my Dad that it was "a right bloody mess inside!" but my Dad responded that our house looked OK from the back. When he went to the door the first comment was that somebody didn't lock the door! Well they had, but the explosion/implosion forced the door open.

When we did go in, oh what a mess! The double casement windows at the front, were blown out and leaning against the fireguard on the opposite side of the room. The front door was halfway up the stairs, the bath was broken and you could see from one bedroom into the other, because their was a quarter inch horizontal gap in the cinderblock wall. Clearly the house was uninhabitable.

While our parents were probably trying to decide what they were going to do, we of course went out looking for shrapnel! What had wrecked our house was a land mine. i.e. It was dropped by parachute and exploded when it hit the ground or anything else. It landed at the corner of Gerald Road & Tabley St. The hole it made was big enough to drop a 2 story house into, but amazingly the people were in an Anderson shelter in the back garden, and weren't killed. I do remember seeing at the bottom of the crater, a Singer sewing machine, just like my Mam's. Across the street from this was a toffee shop, so of course we were looking through the debris for toffees, we did NOT find one. During all this a man climbed up a damaged building to rescue a cat, in the process, he touched a live wire, and the shock sent him all the way to the ground. He didn't die, but we did see him carted off on a door, as no stretcher was available. There were many houses destroyed, and I recall a soldier, obviously coming home on leave, carrying a kit bag on his shoulder, who arrived home to see a leveled piece of ground. Presumably that is where his home had been and he asked if I knew what had happened to the people who lived there! Fortunately I was able to tell him that they weren't killed and that the Air Raid Warden could probably tell him where they had gone. By my reckoning, using old photos, I believe there were 31 houses completely demolished; and lots more made uninhabitable.

Now, what happened to us? Well my Grandad sent Uncle James to the phone box, to phone family in Warrington to see if they could put us up. Before he could give the message, he was interrupted by the operator who told him, that long distance calls, all of 18 miles, were only for emergencies! My Grandad then had a telegram sent which was supposed to say 8 Mathers arriving tonight, unfortunately it had a typo and actually said 8 Mothers!!

That evening we took the bus to Warrington, which I guess must have taken at least 2 hours, because there was a black-out, and the headlamps could only have a thin beam of light about 5" wide and 1 inch high. My Dad had a voucher for our fares, but when the conductor came, he couldn't find the voucher, but the conductor commented, that no-one would do that journey at night with all those children if he didn't have to, and promptly said forget about the fare. I remember having an upset stomach on the bus (I wonder why!!) and my Dad gave me a little sip of Indian Brandy. I don't think it was actually brandy, but rather a patent medicine.

We arrived very late at night, probably about 8'0 clock, and first were bathed by Dorothy Rigby. Tom was very indignant because he thought she was going to try to scrub off the dirty marks on his leg, and said "It won't come off – its a birth mark." So eventually we were sent to bed. Some time later we heard the sirens and did as we were trained. We all had siren suits, something like a "onesie" with a hood. We put them on the floor at the side of the bed so we could get out, put feet in and pull up the suit very quickly.

We quickly trooped downstairs, into the living room and asked where the shelter was. We were told to go back to bed, and they had a hard time convincing us to go! Later my Mam told us that her Uncle Harry had broken down and wept, because he thought it was so sad that little children had to live like that.

I think it must have been the coldest winter on record, and we walked a mile to school, which included going over a very high cantilever bridge where we were subject to the most biting winds. From the bedroom where the boys slept we could see a great big apple tree, and figured we could probably reach it when the fruit came. Well, I think we went home in May, because the house had been repaired by the corporation, so we never got the apples! While we were there we saw a convoy (Tanks, Bren gun carriers, AA guns) which took about 3 hours to pass, never did find out where it was going.

We carried on what to us was a normal life. We built dens out of materiel from bombed houses, we played in bombed houses. One day a friend of mine from school came to our den, and told me a tale of woe. He had been swimming in the canal, the cops came and he ran away, but had forgotten his glasses and was afraid to go home. He thought he would sleep in our den, and asked me if I could get him a marmalade buttie from our house. Sure I could, and went and asked my Mam. "Why do you want that?" she said, "Oh, I'm hungry" – but she knew that I didn't care for marmalade. I imagine she got one of the others (probably Gerard) to find out what was going on, and shortly after Billy MacMullen's Dad appeared to take him home (sans glasses).

As with most childhoods from time to time we had problems with certain neighbours. There was a girl (as old as our Mary) who must have upset me, and in return I called her specky four eyes (cos she wore glasses). My big mistake was that I was near their house, and her mother heard, and came dashing out obviously intending to clip me on the earhole! I ran home, and our back gate had a latch with a striker, and I knew that I could lock it with a nail.....which I did. Her mother had to just stand at the back gate and scream at me, while I safely sat on the back step (probably wearing a cheeky grin).

Some time around then there was a movie called the Sullivans (probably propaganda). It was about 5 brothers who joined the Navy, and throughout the film it showed them always together, but with the youngest one lagging behind. And of course he was always saying "Hey fellers wait for me." At the end the ship got sunk with all hands, and the end of the film showed them up in the clouds wearing halos, four on one cloud, and the youngest on another hollering "Hey fellers wait for me." And I bet you've guessed what's coming. Our James, being the youngest at the time, was told that he had stay quite a bit behind Gerard, Me, Tom, Neville, and furthermore every few minutes he had to holler: "Hey Fellers wait for me!"

Then there was this rotten kid called Keith Phillips. Don't know why we didn't get on with him. One day he hid behind the fence and threw half a brick at me, worse still it hit me and gave me one whopper of a bruise. I think it was around this time that some woman told my Mam, that nobody dare touch your kids, because if they do, they are likely to be set on by a whole army...my Mam thought this was as it should be. Anyway, one morning going to school Me, Tom, Neville, James, and Margaret, we were a bit late because I was carrying Margaret on my shoulders. Mrs Phillips is calling Keith in her high-pitched voice, and every time she called I made a Cock a Doodle Do sound. Of course I thought it was real funny, but she didn't! And she chased us, caught up with us near school and belted me round the ears. She would never have caught us If I hadn't been carrying Margaret as well as our gas masks!

Also while we were at Walsall St, our Mary got diptheria, when she was 7 or 8 so it was probably 1936. She was taken in an ambulance to Ladywell hospital behind Hope……..most times when people were taken in an ambulance you figured they were beyond hope! I remember seeing her put into the ambulance. She was in Ladywell for 7 or 8 weeks in isolation, and my Mam and Aunty Margaret went everyday on the tram and took a parcel, orange or fruit. But they never got to speak to her, and Mary says the food was shared with other children in the hospital. While she was in there she remembers seeing Mrs Garner,(Kevin's Grandma) and waving to her through the window. Also while she was in there our Tom got sick, so my Mam took him to see Dr Becker, who could find nothing wrong with him. The doctor finally came to the conclusion that he was pining for Mary! He was the baby at the time, and Mary had played with him quite a lot.

** Mary's Ladywell Letters are enclosed in the appendix **

Another "Tom" story. At that time we had a sideboard which was quite high (in my mind anyway), and Tom who was about 3 tried climbing up it. He got so far, then fell, landing on a chair, and broke his arm

In 1942 our James was born, and the day he was born Fr Corcoran decided to pay a visit. He walked from church coming in through the back garden, where my Dad was inspecting the tomatoes he had grown in his little greenhouse. Corky's opening comment was something like "How's it going?" My Dad, thinking of his tomatoes said they were coming along fine, then realized that Corky was asking about Mam. Dad told him she had just had a baby boy, and took him in. Fr Corcoran was absolutely amazed he had never seen a baby that was only a few hours old.

I think it was late 1943 that we moved to 47 Broughton Road. My Mam had heard that this house was being renovated after being damaged in the blitz, and she knew the man that owned it (He had a greengrocers shop on Broughton Rd). Mam and Dad were able to rent it, and we moved in. Unlike today, our moving method was a little different. Many things were taken in the pram, a handcart was borrowed and some stuff moved on that. The heavy furniture was moved on Arthur MacMullens coal cart!

After we had moved in, I realized that I'd been around this house before! Troops had been training (probably for the invasion) and were going in all the empty houses. For hand grenades they were using little bags (which had some white substance in them) and of course, when thrown, they didn't always burst. So, naturally, us lads collected the ones that hadn't burst, and joined in the "fun" by throwing our grenades at the soldiers. Poor guys they not only had to do as they were told, but also had to put up with these 'orrible little monsters!

Pauline was the first one born at "47," on the March 11th 1944, which was the day I was notified that I had won a scholarship to De La Salle College (what was later referred to as the 11+ exams.) 47 had 3 bedrooms and a bathroom (bath only, no toilet) upstairs, and Parlour, middle room, and kitchen downstairs. There was also a cellar which had a coal-hole and a room where the "copper" was. This was a copper boiler set into the brickwork, with a grate beneath it where a fire could be lit to heat the water for washing. Just in front of the front door there was a hole which had a metal lid where the coalman dumped the coal.

In the back yard, there was a lavatory, and attached to it was a shelter, with double brick walls and a concrete roof. By then the air raids had stopped and we only used the shelter for storage.........oh, except, that we built a garden on the top. This entailed acquiring bricks from a bombed site, and making a wall about 4 bricks high then filling it with dirt. We did not have a ladder, and so, got on to the roof by climbing, a bit tricky when you have a bucketful of dirt (probably 20 buckets full) and also carrying all the bricks up. And all this so we could grow some radishes and lettuce.......mind you we also had an allotment (more about that later) but that was a mile away. The rest of the yard was used at various time to keep rabbits(pets) and at one time to fatten up a cockerel (in a tea chest).

The boys slept in the front bedroom, the girls in the back, and Mam and Dad in the middle bedroom. I think there were eventually 2 single beds in the girls room, one of which my Dad made. He bought the wood (don't know where cos there were no wood stores that we were aware of) and carried it home strapped to the crossbar of his bicycle. He also bought angle iron, took it to work where he drilled the holes so it could be assembled. You have to realize that mattresses at that time were flock mattresses, and I think they were laid on metal straps that looked like lattice work.

While this book is primarily about the "happenings" in the house I think it only right that details of the house itself should be included. The house was built sometime around 1875- 1880. In the early 40s it was owned by Mr Gregory who was a greengrocer on Broughton Rd, and it was damaged by the land mine which fell on London St school. Sometime in 1943 my Mam heard that it was being repaired and would be rented out. She approached Mr Gregory and was successful in renting the house, and so we moved in....at the time there was Mam and Dad and seven children. Somewheres around 1954 we heard that Mr Gregory was thinking of selling it which caused great consternation. I took it upon myself to go to talk to him, pointing out that there was a large crack in the back wall and that surely as "sitting tenants" my Mam and Dad should get a reduced price. He agreed that they could have it for 200 pounds (which clearly was a worthwhile reduction because Harry Marshall our neighbour paid 450 pounds for theirs).

Later in this book it describes how and where my Dad got the mortgage and the house was bought in my mom's name.... life goes on, and in 1958 I moved to Canada. While I was there I was sent the Salford Reporter and became aware that the City was replanning the whole area and "47" was just about the middle of that quadrant. I was concerned, and wrote to the corporation expressing my concerns, and suggesting that my parents should get replacement value as the value of their house was already diminished because of the destruction of the surrounding neighbourhood and they replied with the usual gobbledy gook that they were aware. Perhaps a year later my Mam phoned on a Sunday night and told me that the house was sold. I asked how much and was given a figure that was about half of what would be needed to buy a similar house, and suggested she says, only to be told its too late, its done. Obviously I was some upset, and said "Well I'll do something" Mam: "What can you do from there!" To which I replied "I'll write to the Queen, that's what I'll do! " Which got my mom's famous "hmmmph."

Well I immediately sat down, wrote the letter, and posted it in case I should change my mind.

MY MAM

A.E. Martin,
510 Third Street,
New Westminster, B.C.,
Canada.

7th June 1973.

Corporation of City of Salford,
Town Hall,
Salford, Lancashire,
England.

Dear Sirs:

Having just read a recent issue of the Salford Reporter (apropos the "slums" of London Street) and as my parents live on the corner of London Street and Broughton Road, I thought I would write to you.

I persuaded my parents to buy that house at a time when many Salford people of their upbringing were not accustomed to the idea of owning their own home. Since they bought it, it has been improved and well maintained.

Both my parents have lived in Salford all their lives and have raised a family (of twelve) there. My Father, particularly, has been active in the community having served on the board of the P.C.I.S., including some time as the President. They have both been active in church activities and to my mind (yes, I'm biased) have served their community well.

Now their home is to be acquired by the City by "compulsory purchase".

I am writing to ask that somebody on your council please look and ensure that they do not get ill-treated in their retirement.

The value of their property, with the demolition of the past few years, has undoubtedly gone down. However, this is not their fault and is due to a long term plan of the City's. I believe that they should get REPLACEMENT VALUE for their house. That is, sufficient money to purchase outright at current values, a three bedroom home with sufficient funds to cover real estate and/or solicitor's fees and removal expense. This may or may not be the usual thing to do, but it would be just and honourable.

If the money offered by the corporation is not sufficient for them to buy a home of their own, or forces them to incur another mortgage at this time of their lives, I would be very disappointed. I do not wish to stand in the way of progress, however I do not wish to see it at the expense of my parents.

My parents, Mr. & Mrs. F. Martin, 47 Broughton Road, Salford 6, do not know about this letter, but I will send them a copy.

Yours truly,

A.E. Martin.

TALES OF FORTY-SEVEN

CITY OF SALFORD

G. Alexander McWilliam, M.A., B.Sc., C.Eng.,
F.I.C.E., F.R.I.C.S., F.I.Mun.E.,
City Engineer, Surveyor & Planning Officer,
Town Hall,
Salford,
M3 6DH

Your Ref. Our Ref. V/SW/JR/4542 Tel. 061-834 2363 Ext. 351

21st June 1973

Dear Sir,

City of Salford (London Street Clearance
Areas 1A/1G) Compulsory Purchase Order 1972 -
47 Broughton Road, Salford 6.

I refer to your letter dated 7th June 1973, and write to advise you on the position with regard to your parents' home, which is affected by the above Order.

The compensation to be paid for the acquisition of the property will be assessed in accordance with current legislation, notably the Land Compensation Act 1973.

This Act brings about important changes in compensation law, including, in addition to the existing entitlement to market value of the property in your parents' case, an entitlement to a 'home loss payment' based on the rateable value of the property, with a minimum of £150.

In view of your concern and the changes in law mentioned above, I have arranged for your parents to discuss the matter with one of my Valuation Assistants.

I trust that this information will reassure you in the concern which you understandably express in your letter.

Yours faithfully,

City Engineer & Surveyor.

A. E. Martin, Esq.,
510 Third Street,
New Westminster, B.C.,
Canada.

MY MAM

Having more or less forgotten about it, I was surprised some time later when my wife Heather phoned me at work and read a letter from my Mam, and what she had written went something like this:

'I was out at the cworp and when I came home one of the children (actually it was Angela Dereume from Canada who's living at 47 at the time) said someone from the Town Hall phoned, and want you to phone him.' Instead of phoning, Mam trots off to the Town Hall and when she gets there, instead of the usual Yeh well wait there a minute she is greeted with "Oh yes Mrs Martin, come in, sit down."

Then it starts:

Official: "What's this then, ave you been writing to the Queen?"

Mam starting to snicker: "No I've not."

Off: "It's nothing to laugh at, this is very serious, there's been questions in the "Ouses of Parliament" phone calls from Buckingham Palace. Do you know who did write?"

"Yes it's one of my sons"... "What did he write"... "I don't know..I know what he wrote to the corporation"...

Off: "We know that, we've got a copy but we don't know what he wrote to the Queen...do you have any other children"...

"Yes I've got twelve!"

"Bloody Ell!"

He then asked why I'd written and my Mam went on to explain that she had a daughter in Chippenham, one in Canada, and a son in Canada and when they came to visit they expected to stay with their parents and they can't do that in a one bedroom flat in a highrise that you are offering. He asked further questions such as what did I do in Canada to which my Mam having only a vague idea about my job, said:

"Oh, he's the accountant at the State Penitentiary...." "hmm I bet he's got a nice house"... "yes he has." She also added that I'd written because I thought they were diddling her.

Well I got a response from a lady in waiting to the Queen, which didn't really offer very much more, although my Mam did get a bit more money. However what she did get instead of a one bedroom flat in a high rise on Ellor St (which eventually turned into slums, where the lifts did not work) was a three bedroom house, with a garden back and front, on a bus route for a very low rent (it was on Overdale in Swinton)

Some years later my Mam told me that a lady who worked for the City told her: "You know what happened Mary...It's that letter from your Anthony to the Queen..they'll never give you a hard time"...which made me feel good and left visions in my mind of a file somewhere with a big notice on it saying: Handle with Care..rotten kid writes to the Queen!

And now to Joe's original idea for this book: Tales of "47!" and oh dear, how many there are!

When we arrived, behind "47" the houses had been bombed, flattened and most of the rubble cleared away, so it was like a croft. A wonderful playground for us!

At some time the government had a policy of encouraging people to have "Holidays at Home" right up our street (cause we couldn't generally afford to go anywhere). There was a pile of sand there, residue from some construction thing. We used to make cities of sand, play with dinky toys there, and one day discovered a lead pipe in the ground. Now it could very well have been a gas pipe, but lucky for us it was a water pipe, and we soon discovered that we could chop into it with an axe and have a river, and at night simply closed it by hitting it with a hammer. This went on for several weeks, until somebody in the corporation got wise and turned off the water somewhere! Rotters!

We also played cricket using the lamp as the wicket, and although we had been told umpteen dozen times not to play football on London St, but to go to the croft, we must have forgotten, (ahem!) At this time Uncle Eddie had come back from the war, where he had been in Egypt/Palestine, and brought us back a real leather football! One day I was playing, shooting the ball against the wall, between the two windows of the middle room, anyway I took this terrific shot, and as soon as it left my foot I knew it was going to hit one of the windows! Grandad Eagleton (who was in one of the photos from Formby) said "Good Shot Anthony!" And then as the glass broke, there was this bloodcurdling scream, as our Mary was in the middle room playing records and I guess, understandably, was surprised – shocked – scared!

However she wasn't as scared as me, because I knew I was in BIG TROUBLE. Of course I went in, and very quickly became tired and said I was going to bed (My Dad wasn't home yet). I went to bed, and pretended to sleep, while shivering with fear for what I'd done and what would happen to me. Well, inevitably, my Dad came home from the club, came upstairs and asked me if I wanted to take my punishment now, or wait till tomorrow. I thought best get it over with, and said now. He took me out on to the landing, and he had this branch of a tree with knots in it, and then gave me an opportunity. Do you want to take your punishment now, or do you want to pay for the window? Looking at this horrible branch, I opted to pay for the window. Then I went to bed, and realised I'd been conned! He would never have hit me with that (he certainly wasn't vicious). And in any case I didn't have any money, which he knew. Unbeknown to me, but learned later from my Mam, that he went downstairs, breathed a sigh of relief, telling Mam, "I didn't know what I was going to do when Anthony said he'd take his punishment now." Then told her he'd had a brainwave and offered to let me pay for the window. In later years when Mam visited us we had many laughs about that.

One December around the end of World War 2, two men came to our house. I would be around 11 and knew these men. One was John Dolly (an apparitor at church ... which means he took the collection plate around) and the other Jim Wood the caretaker from St Sebastians school. They were invited in and us children were told to go outside and play. When we returned it was apparent that my mother was very happy, but some tears had been shed, but then life went on.

Now moving on about 45 yrs, my Mam now in her 80s had been sick and was somewhat frail. My brothers and sisters had to go back to work after Christmas, and were concerned about leaving her on her own, so my wife and I volunteered to go to England for a month & look after her. This is one of the things we learned. At that time my parents had about 8 children, and had no money for a turkey, or to help Father Christmas with his duty(and we always at least got a book). The men were from the St Vincent de Paul society and gave her ten pounds(which was probably the equivalent of 2 weeks wages) for my Dad. She believed that the money had come from her father, who believed that you should not be seen to favour one child over another (common thinking at that time), so he got round it by giving via the SVP.

When my grandfather died he left each of his grand-children (including those conceived but not yet born) Five pounds. This was another way in which he was able to leave a bit more money to those of his children who had families, a little extra.

When Heather & I came back to England, to look after my Mam, it was in our minds that we were doing a good turn for others, but in truth, we were the greatest beneficiaries, because we learned so much. Here are a couple of other stories my Mam told us:

We knew that Mam had met Dad when on a church outing to the Lake District, but I knew she didn't go on that trip with him, , so I asked her, saying you didn't go on that trip with my Dad but with another chap, what happened with him..

She answered by saying "He exposed himself" Well you never think of your parents in a sexual manner, and I was completely dumbfounded with this revelation,, and when I recovered from the shock all I could think of to say, was "What did you do"............ "I slapped his face!"

Of course we never told anybody about this at the time, but years later on another trip, I told Gerard first, and subsequently some of the others. When I told Margaret, she said with a laugh... "I bet his face still hurts!"

Another story she told: She had been shopping at the "cworp" and when she came home there was a little old lady sitting on the front door step shivering. She was scruffy and dirty,and cold.. Nonetheless my Mam invited her in and gave her some hot soup and a cup of tea, and sat her by the fireplace to warm up. (I honestly wonder what I would have done in the circumstances). The lady then proceeded to tell Mam her story. At one time she had had a good job and was secretary to a mill-owner. She eventually became his mistress, and he set her up in a flat and promised to look after her. Well, unfortunately for her, he had a heart attack and died suddenly. His wife apparently knew about this relationship, and promptly fired her, and suggested to all the other mill-owners that they not hire her. She eventually had no means of support and became what was known as a bag woman. She lived halfway up Shuttleworth street, and when she died it took 3 men (dressed in paper overalls) almost a week to empty & dis-infect the house, which was full of rubbish, tons of newspapers and she also had cats in there. When I told this story to my siblings years later, my sister Angela said "I remember that!" She had come home from school for lunch, my Mam told her to get her lunch and go back to school. Angela told us that the lady smelled terribly and was dirty & scruffy, and of course as a young child, Angela wondered what was going on. Just another example of how good our mother was!

"47" had been damaged by another land mine which hit a nearby school (London St School), and my Dad actually saw the land mine coming down on its parachute (from a distance fortunately). It destroyed most of the school as well as about 5 blocks of nearby houses, but left one corner of the school (2 or 3 stories high) still standing! There was also a house in the corner of the yard, presumably the caretaker's house, and that didn't get damaged..or not very much. Also the ARP (Air Raid Precaution) wardens gathering point was not destroyed. Well the bit that was still standing, was quite a challenge to us, and when we weren't playing soldiers in the nearby trenches, we were throwing stones, trying to smash the few remaining windows on the top floor (it was very difficult!).

Close to this school was what we called the croft, (Vic's field) there had been a tip – (rubbish dump) there at one time and we used to play football, cricket etc. there. Well one day there were some other kids playing cricket there, and some fellows playing pitch & toss (an illegal gambling game). All of a sudden several police cars appeared, cops jumped out and chased the fellows to arrest them! One chap was VERY smart. As soon as the cops appeared, he went & stood behind the wicket (as if he had been playing with the kids)........the cops missed him!

When we first moved into Broughton Rd., the building opposite (which eventually became Harry Marshall's) was at that time a firewood manufactory, owned by a Malteser (no not a chocolate, but a chap who comes from Malta), his name was Charlie, and his horses name was Samson. Clearly we were far more interested in the horse. This man had a great big circular saw – about 2 ft in diameter. He used to go and salvage beams from bombed houses, saw them into lengths of about 8 inches. Then they were split with an axe, and he had a jig that you could put the pieces in, tighten it up and wrap it with wire. This was sold for kindling. We (Gerard and me, and possibly Tom) used to go in there and help him making up the bundles, but I don't remember ever getting paid. I think we went in there for a chance to pet Samson! There was another man at the end of our block, who also had a horse and cart, but he was a miserable one. His name was Knight and he was a Rag and Bone man. I will explain for the uninitiated. He went round with his horse & cart, collecting rags (yes any kind of dirty old rags). In exchange you would get brown or white stone (a cake of chalk-like substance which was used for cleaning and colouring) the flagstones, or steps in front of the house. For houses where the front door opened right on to the street, this was very important to many women. On occasion, you could sometimes get a gold fish (but you had to supply your own jam-jar!).

I'm sure some readers will wonder why he collected rags. The reason is that they could be sold for making paper. Not very far from "47" there was a chimney stack which always belched dirty grey smoke – this was where the rags were cleaned, and baled, prior to being sent to the paper manufacturer.

I mentioned earlier that my Dad didn't have much formal education (which is probably why he sacrificed so much to ensure that we, his children did). He did not, however let his lack of education hold him back, and at some time in the late 40s early 50s there was an effort made to try to get more Catholics involved at different levels of government. Thus my Dad was asked to put up for election to the board of Pendleton Co-op. He agreed, and when the votes were counted, he "topped the poll".

He did this for altruistic reasons, but eventually he realized there were some advantages. The Chairman of the Board (James Woolley, J.P.) seemed to be impressed with Dad's determination to do things properly. He was on the board for several years, and at one time he was asked to be the tour leader (with my Mam) on a coach trip. He didn't have to pay, but obviously everyone else did. I think it was 10 or 14 days and they went to the south coast. I know they stayed in Brighton in the best hotel,(which many years later was damaged by a bomb that was intended to kill Margaret Thatcher) and also Bognor Regis. Our parents never, ever dreamed that they would be staying in such posh surroundings.

Perhaps this is where I should insert one of the funny things (co-op related). Gerard, Me, Tom (and possibly Neville) tied a rope to the bannister upstairs, and jumped off about the seventh stair. The aim of the game was to see if you could touch the light bulb hanging from the lobby ceiling, and often we did!

We did NOT know that this stopped the bulb from working. We also didn't know until much later that Dad had gone to the co-op manager and suggested he change their bulb supplier, because he had had 3 or 4 bulbs wear out in just a few weeks!

It would also be in this time frame when the iron curtain was installed. We never knew why this operation was carried out, and can only think that it was a "make-work" option to try to keep us out of mischief. My Dad belonged to St Sebastian's Working Men's club, of which one of the founders was Ted Mather, which besides having billiards tables, place to play crib etc also had a bar. This gave access to loads of beer bottle tops (probably thousands!). So we were each given a 6 inch nail, a block of wood and a hammer. The younger ones were given something to pry out the cork and the silver paper lining out of the top first. Then we took the tops, placed them on the wooden block and made a hole in them with the nail.

I'm guessing that from the landing to the floor was probably 8 feet, and the width of the stairway perhaps 3 feet 6 inches. There had to be at least 30 of these strings of bottle tops. They were hung from a rod from the ceiling which was at one time the rack on which incendiary bombs hung, which was found on Robinson's front step on the morning after the blitz. Robinson's were our next door neighbour in Walsall St, and Pat Robinson married George Garner (Kevin's uncle).

On 5 July 1945, baby number 9 arrived, and it was a boy When he was named, the boys all wanted a "real" name, not anything fancy. Mary wanted Gregory (I thought it was because she liked Gregory Peck), and so he got the moniker Gregory John, and for many years was always called by both names (which satisfied the boys and the girls). When he was about 9 months old, he got very sick during the night, and Mam and Dad got up, walked to Salford Royal Hospital (approximately two miles) and John was operated on immediately, the surgeon having said that if our parents had not taken him, he would have been dead in the morning! It seems he had a twisted bowel, and once again my Mam's dedication to her children came into play. Every day she walked to the hospital, at least twice, to feed John! I don't recall how long he was in, but it must have been at least 10 days.

While he was in there, there was a baby girl who had to be operated on because she had some eggshell stuck in her throat. I'm sure you can imagine the care taken in cooking eggs, AND in inspecting same when it landed on your plate. and I'm sure this lasted quite a long time at "47". Also around this time, Jimmy Johns (who married aunty Kath) came up from Cornwall. He used to go rabbiting, using ferrets, and later using a greyhound which Grandad Ted Mather got from Albion dog track. Well on this trip, he brought 2 very small baby rabbits, so small they would both have fitted in a strawberry punnet. Of course they finished up at 47, and until a hutch was made they lived in the fireplace (inside the fender). Eventually, they were allowed into the (miniscule) front garden, and when Mam said to them "get in!" they always obeyed. One time a kid knocked at our front door and told us that a cat had picked one of them up and ran down the entry across the street. The lads of course followed, climbed over back doors, and eventually found the rabbit, scared stiff, sitting in an empty (thankfully) gazunder,(for those who don't know it's called a gazunder because it goes under the bed i.e a poe, jerry, chamber pot) from where he was returned home.

We had other animals, one of which was a big ginger cat. On occasion this would follow Mam down London St when she was going for the rations, and if it got as far as the dinner centre, she would turn round and tell the cat to, "Go on home!" and it did! Unfortunately, this poor animal came to a sad end, and got run over by a car, right outside our front door. Of course any animal that died got a funeral at our house, and this one was buried under a small rose bush outside the front window. Now that rose was the only plant we had brought from 15 Walsall St, cause my Dad treasured it. In Walsall St it never had more than 4 blooms. After the cat was interred it regularly had 100 and more blooms! Of course in later years I used to tell my children that cats were good for roses (only if they were buried under the rose) and after reading this, my children will know why I teased them this way.

On May 8th 1945 we celebrated VE(Victory in Europe) Day. We celebrated this by having the biggest bonfire of all time, and the fire was in the middle of London St right by our house. You should realize, that there were still loads of bombed houses around and so there was practically an unlimited supply of wood, and instead of Guy Fawkes we burned Adolf Hitler. The fire lasted 3 days!

Another item from this era was the allotment. An allotment was a piece of ground, which could be rented for a very low payment, and would be used for growing food (to supplement the "rations"). Our allotment was about 1 mile from the house (and of course we had to walk, there and back). There was a well on the property (you had to lower a bucket on a rope many times) to water the garden. Nowadays instructions that come with seed packages say something like plant the seeds in a row and after they have sprouted, thin them out. Our instruction came from my Dad and Grandad, and I remember planting radish seeds, ONE at a time, (no thinning out needed). I recall one day when there were several of us at the allotment, Me, Tom, Neville, Joe-Ed (cousin), and Gerard. My Grandad had an 8ft long cane (Intended for holding netting to grow peas), and I remember the others having what amounted to a free ride, because he concentrated on ME, prodding me with the cane saying "Come on lad, you can do better (or quicker) than that....don't be lazy!" Meanwhile the rest are having a quiet snicker cause I'm the one that's being harassed! When I later complained to my Mam, she only replied, he loves you, and in any case he can see himself in you!

Victory in Europe day was in May 1945 – so the European war was over, even though the war in the far East was still going on. In (I think) August of 1945 it was decided that the Lancashire Royal Agricultural Show would take place on Littleton Road Playing Fields. So shortly before that, on a Sunday after dinner I decided to go out. Asked where I was going said that I was going up to Littleton Road to see if I could get a job at the Show. "Good idea Anthony, go to it' with the unspoken inference – Fat chance, but have a go." So off I went. On my return, I called in at No 1 to tell my Grandad what had happened, and it went like this:

Man: What you up to young feller?
Anthony: I'm looking for a job

The man replied that he could give me one, but could I get 5 more boys to help. Well I certainly could! The job was to go around and collect all the empty pop bottles (days before deposits and recycling). Then he asked how much I wanted paying (which rather dumbfounded me – after all I was only 12), and then asked if 7/6d a day would be enough, to which (although being over the moon inside) I said oh yes I think that will do. This was to work Friday, Saturday, Sunday Monday; then I told him I couldn't be there till early afternoon on Sunday, the reason being I was going to Mass, and he said that was Ok because he was going as well.

I then went home, was asked if I got a job, and was very pleased to be able to tell them, Yes, and for Gerard, Tom Ed, Joe Ed, and two more lads. It was my parents turn to be surprised! Years later my Mam told me that my Grandad was very proud of me and bragging about me – but that was mostly because of telling the man I wouldn't go till after Mass! There was a sequel to this. I was supposed to go back the next week, but Harry Marshall offered a trip to Rhyll, and I was wondering what to do. Mam said, Oh go to Rhyll, Gerard will go to talk to the man. I did, and Gerard did, and as a result he got to be the boss and got ten shilling a day instead of 7/6d. Anyway we were all very happy at being paid a fortune(to us), while at the same time having access to everywhere in the show, and as much free crisps and ginger ale as we wanted! I think they lost money on us!

There was a cockerel that we (I) fattened up to eat. It was kept in a tea chest, and when it got to the size that it could be eaten, well then obviously it had to be slaughtered (does "killed" sound better?). Well, my Dad wasn't going to do it, and nobody else seemed keen, so I volunteered. I guess I would have been about 12 at that time, and had seen where grown men killed chickens, hens etc, by gripping the neck between the first and second fingers of both hands, and twisting. Well, they were grown men, and I certainly wasn't, and no matter how I twisted it wouldn't work and the cock kept crowing!

So, let's try something else. In those days we thought we had an axe, but I have since realized it was really a wedge used to split logs, furthermore, it was far from sharp. Sorry to say, it took a long time and many whacks with the so-called axe before the cockerel finally succumbed. (I think I finally cut off its head with the bread knife) I know, you are thinking how could anyone be that cruel, but it really was a different way of life and poultry was hard to come by. Well the bird was plucked, then cooked, and then half of the family couldn't think of eating something they saw in the yard, every time they went to the loo!

I should have known better, because when we kept chickens in Walsall St. my Dad wouldn't kill them either, and I had to take them down to MacMullens for him to do it.

Interruption!

During the war (I know it was more than 60 yrs ago) the BBC would sometimes interrupt a programme on the wireless (radio) with the phrase: we interrupt this programme to bring you important news – which could be sad (sinking of a battleship) exciting (Montgomery & the Desert Rats winning the battle of El Alamein). So I decided to use this process to interrupt this chapter.

August 2015

At the time of writing, my family and I have just returned from a wonderful holiday in England which included the "Cousins" party (also attended by Elders and young children). My purpose is not to talk about the party, but rather to pay tribute to that wonderful couple who were responsible for all of us being there......Yes, Mam and Dad Martin. Without their sacrifices this Unique, fun loving, laughing family would not exist, and including them it now covers 5 generations! So take a break, raise your glass, and drink a toast to Mary and Frank Martin!!!

Now back to the stories!

While we were living at Walsall St. Our big deal of the year was to be taken the circus at Belle Vue. One year (for us lads) the big attraction was the knife thrower. So at the first available opportunity (which means when my Mam was out of the house), Gerard and me "persuaded" Tom to stand at the back door while we threw knives at him, well close to him! Lucky for us we didn't hit him but what we did do was break the knife. Now you must realize that the door was 2 inches thick oak, and a throwing knife probably wouldn't penetrate much less an eating knife which didn't even have a point! So we quickly stopped the game and went and buried the broken knife in the garden hoping it wouldn't be missed, and it wasn't. There was however a sequel to this story! Some time later we were washing dishes and Tom was drying and he broke one of the cups. At that time the cups were "utility" cups, no proper handle, but a kind of wedge stuck on where the handle should be. Of course Gerard and I started to wind Tom up, saying "ha ha ha! You'll have to pay for it!" Quite stupid really cos we had no money. However Tom put an end

INTERRUPTION!

to this nonsense by saying, "Mam, how much would you have to pay if you broke a knife?" Well of course we shut up very quickly and either my Mam didn't hear us, or she ignored us!

And of course not much happens that Mary doesn't
celebrate it with a rhyme.
One day, Dad was digging in the garden,
at the back,
Intent on building an Anderson shelter;
a handy little shack
Where we would spend so many nights in bunks that
Dad had made.
For he was very handy with hammer, nails, and
spade.

Suddenly he hit something. He thought he'd hit
it rich.
With this object he had found digging in the ditch.
It's bound to be some roman treasure,
buried here for years.
Now at last he could pay rent which was always
in arrears.

He picked it up and cleaned it off, and there beneath
the dirt,
He found the broken kitchen knife.
Mam was feeling hurt,
A wedding present from great gran.
Mam was right to be upset.
I'll bet I know who's guilty.
She was right, she won that bet.

*A family meeting soon was called, to find the one
who knew
Exactly what had happened. Dad said,
"Anthony was it you?"
He knew where to lay the blame upon the lad who
had no shame.
Always in trouble was his claim to fame.
The lion tamers at Belle Vue would rent him
for a bob or two
To see if trainees could subdue the leader of our
motley crew.
He likened it to being in a cage, with roaring lions
in a rage.
To Anthony, this was nothing more than enjoying
being centre stage.
Well Anthony thought it over and decided to come
clean.
He'd give his version of events,
He wouldn't make a scene.
After all, there were others in this scheme, and
he could name them all.
So could big sister Mary, she could put him
in his stall.
"Well you see Dad, it's like this, we learned it
at Belle Vue.
We thought it looked easy, that we could do it too.
So we stood Tom up by the back door.
(a gentle soul was he)
Then we began to throw the knives.
Thats how it was you see.*

INTERRUPTION!

We'd not been living at 47 very long when Tom, Gerard, and I went to the pictures (at the ambassador). That day a lad at school (Frank Thornton) had given me a cigarette, (never had one of these before) so after we came out of the pictures I tore it in two ,gave Gerard half, we lit them and walked along Eccles Old Road smoking. There used to be some steps near the corner of Langworthy Rd and Eccles Old Rd, and we had just passed them. Me smoking like George Lockhart (the Ringmaster at Belle Vue Circus) and his cigar and Gerard being older and smarter had hidden his in his hand. All of a sudden I'm picked up, held up in the air (seemed like 20 feet to me). I'd been nicked by two well known salford detectives, one of them used to be referred to as "babyface." First he asked my name and address to which I replied: Norman Coleman, I live at 47 Blandford Rd (absolute lies), and of course when he said, "Oh we've had him before" and I said that wasn't my name, then he said, "oh you tell lies too!" Well it was only a few yards so they took me to the police station (and probably had the time of their lives asking all kinds of useless questions). When they had had enough fun I was made to sit in a room where I could see a cell, and I was blubbering and the sergeant told me to shut up or he'd belt me! Eventually after several hours (to me) probably 15 minutes they let me go. Now you may think that Roger Bannister did the first 4 minute mile, well you are wrong. It was me! I ran from there hollering GERARD! TOM! And finally caught up with them near the blank wall just before 47. I suspect they had been dragging their feet so they wouldn't have to explain my absence. That would have been about 1944, and my parents didn't hear about it until 1964 when I came back from Canada on a visit and all the lads were in the kitchen reminiscing, while my

Mam was apparently dozing in her rocking chair. She'd suddenly open one eye and mutter, "hmmm I hadn't heard that before". Another thing we used to do at "47," mostly Tom and I, was to take the train fro Pendleton Station to Clifton Junction and go on the tip picking coal. We also took the trolley t the Gas works to get coke; for the younger end, thats something that was burnt in the fireplace, not snorted up the nose!

There was a policeman in our neighbourhood, who was in the same class as Gerard at De La Salle, his name was Bernard Amos, and very close to Christmas he called at our house, and spoke to my Mam, telling her that a shop on Broad St had asked if he knew of any large families that could use a Christmas Tree, and he named our family. So Tom and I were volunteered to go and collect the tree. At this point you should understand that up to this time our Christmas tree was an imitation one about 2 feet high, and probably 20 yrs old. Tom and I went for the tree, it was HUMONGOUS! Well it was at least 8 ft tall, and what's more they gave us the decorations as well. We went home and it was set up in the front room. I learned an added bit about it just a couple of weeks ago! When Angela (who I think would be about 5 at the time) saw it she said to my Dad "Where did that come from ?" My Dad replied, "If you stand in just the right place, at just the right time, it comes out of the sky, and lands right in front of you!!" Angela tells me she believed that for years!

Reminiscenses

Before writing this tome, I had written to my siblings asking for their memories. It now seems an appropriate time to include their stories (bear in mind that much of what has been written, has come from discussions with others, but what follows is exactly as it was sent to me).

(From Pete)

A memorable Christmas. I think it must have been 1957, I was nine years old then. I decided I would buy everyone in the house a present to go under the Christmas tree (narrators note – the one that Angela thought dropped from the sky -probably!)I can't remember most of them but I do remember buying you 5 Players Cigarettes (I can't believe they allowed a 9 year old to buy cigarettes) but I also bought some candy cigarettes. I put your cigs in the candy cigs packet but it would only hold four so I put a little note inside telling you that I had the fifth one in a safe place. The only other one that I remember was a package of Murraymints for our Tom. (the significance of Murraymints is that Tom was very thorough and could not be hurried, and there was a radio commercial which sang Murraymints, Murraymints the too good to hurry mints!)

The milk was kept behind the front door so when we needed a fresh bottle we had to walk up the lobby, pick up a bottle of milk, walk back down the lobby, open the kitchen door, step down to the kitchen.................then at this point it was necessary to lean on the door because me Dad had put a spring on it but because there were about 20 coats hanging on the door it was too heavy for the spring to close it properly. Well I had worked out a little routine where I would step down to the kitchen(just one step), lean away from the door on one leg till it was returned to the closed position then sway back on the other leg in perfect time to lean on the door to "push it to" (close it properly). This was a really comfortable routine for me, a bit like a ritual dance that I quite enjoyed performed and didn't mind going down the cold lobby, from the warm kitchen to get the milk. Then one day me Dad decided to remove the spring from the door – nobody told me! Consequently I walked up the lobby, picked up a fresh bottle of milk, walked back down the lobby, leaned over on my front leg, leaned back in perfect time to going headlong up the lobby with the milk splashing all over me and the lobby!

Big decision, lets decorate the front bedroom, said me Mam. Beds were dismantled and taken into the front parlour and several of us slept down there – no idea for how long but one night when we were down there me Mam and Dad went out for the night. This was quite a rare occurrence from what I can remember and when they came home somebody had put the "sneck" on the front door so me Mam and Dad were locked out. They came home and tried the door – nope. They tried ringing the door bell and knocking on the door – nope. But the window in the parlour wasn't quite shut so they pushed it up and, presumably me Dad, (I bet it wasn't says Anthony) climbed into the parlour, struggling to avoid the beds. They may have avoided the beds but they didn't manage to avoid the tadpole that were in a bowl on the window ledge. I have vague recollections of people trying to pick up the tadpoles and put them back in the bowl. There was another incident some months later when I went down the cellar to get some coal. As you know there was a light (probably about 40 watts – not very bright) near where we used to fill the shovel with coal. As I was pushing the shovel under the coal I saw these eyes looking at me from an enormous "beetle". I dropped the shovel and ran up the cellar steps screaming to me Mam, "Mam there's a big black (coal dust but still shiny) beetle in the cellar. After checking out the cellar me Mam asked derek Marshal from next door to come in and shift the frog!

I didn't always appreciate me Dad's sense of humour. Picture the scene, it's chucking it down outside, definitely NOT the kind of day to be playing outside. The hands on the clock are sedately sliding towards the time that me Dad gets home from work. I am sitting on the rocking chair in front of a warm fire that I have tended with great care and it is now breathing red warming heat in my direction. I hear the front door open. I listen to me Dad putting his bike into place in the front lobby and dread the next 40 – 50 seconds. Me Dad pokes his head round the door, takes his sodden cap from his head, puts it in his right arm then swings his arm in an arc, causing what felt like gallons of water to be propelled towards me in the form of a drenching shower. I hope it isn't raining tomorrow!

One winter day. It had been snowing and Vic's hills resembled a mild and very short ski slope, not that I had an inkling of what a ski slope looked like in 1957. Me and John had been out on the hill having a go on other peoples sledges when we could get a ride or just sliding down the slopes. There were three slopes in all; the first was very mild and was not far away from London Street and faced the left hand end of Charlestown Library as you looked at it from the hills. The next one was further along and faced the Cromwell. This was much steeper and anybody sledging went loads further than on the "nursery" slope. The third one was a bit dangerous really. It was at right angles to the one previously described and faced Blandford Road. It was the steepest of the three slopes but there wasn't much of a "run" once you reached the bottom so you could hit all kinds of obstacles from high tufts of frozen grass, a dip in the ground or any old rubbish that had been left around.

We went home for a warm up and took our coats off. We were telling anyone who would listen (I can't imagine anybody could ignore us the way we were talking) how good the sledging was and that the runs on each slope had turned to ice; if only we had our own sledge we could have loads of rides down the slopes. We carried on like this for some time and our Anthony got so fed up with us disturbing the peace in the warm and cosy back kitchen that he grabbed some wood and nails and in no time at all, made us our very own sledge – and it turned out to be a belter. It was very light and had two wooden runners and we frequently out-distanced the "smarter" opposition sledges that had been bought from shops!

That Man
(From "Our Pete")

One night I was just watching all the activity in the back kitchen – there was plenty to watch, I just watched for ages from my favourite vantage point, the rocking chair. (This was during the time when mi Dad would come home from work, have his tea then go upstairs, get washed and changed and to the Co-op for a board meeting). It must have been an hour or so later that I asked mi Mam, "D'you know that man that comes in on a bike and is wearing overalls and a cap, is it the same man that comes in again with a white shirt and tie on and goes out again?

I dot no 'ankerchief

I must have always had a runny nose, still happens. Our table was positioned along the wall of the kitchen and there were chairs on three sides but a bench at the back so that "little uns" could squash together more easily. We had to climb on to the bench one at a time after queuing up behind the door. There must have been a period of time when our Gerard stood at the start of the bench and sort of inspected us as we climbed on to it. I don't know how many times it happened but he always told me to blow my nose and I always replied, "I dot no 'ankerchief' which I "sang" – through a stuffed up nose> When this had happened several times I was ready to climb on the bench and he asked the usual question and the whole family replied in unison, "I dot no ankerchief". This must have made an impression on me because the next time he asked his usual question – then answered it himself, I was able to say "I AVE!"

Eagletons from Rockley Street

At one point in my young life I had what became to me quite a lucrative job. The Co-op bread van used to come around every morning and mi Mam would buy whatever bread she needed and then buy another loaf for 'The Eagletons" This was because the bread van only came down the main road and was not allowed to go up the side streets and the Eagletons lived in Rockley Street. At this time the Eagletons consisted of Grandad, Nellie and Nellie's sister (whose name escapes me at the minute). For delivering their bread daily I received the princely sum of 1d which I was given on Saturday when I received the full 6d.

The Boys' Bedroom
(From "Our Pete")

One night me and our John were having a pillow fight in the bedroom. Our John swung wildly with his pillow and missed but did hit the light that was hung in the centre of the room from the ceiling. There was a "Mothax" ring (like a big polo mint but lavender in colour and smell} hanging from the nightshade and I grabbed it to stop the light from swinging. Me and John both screamed and jumped when the wire that was between the ceiling and the light fitting snapped causing a big and noisy, flash and four balls of flame leapt away from the wire in four directions. Mi Dad came running up the stairs, "What's going ' on?" I told him that as I was steadying the lightshade that had been nudged when we were walking across the bed. Mi Dad didn't seem too convinced but mi Mam came in and pointed out, "Oh Frank we know that wire is old and has needed replacing for a while." Mi Mam worked her magic once again.

On another occasion in the bedroom I was wrestling with our John. We did this quite often when we pretended to be Jackie Pallow or Mick McManus (TV wrestlers at the time). On this occasion, our John ended up sitting on my face and was laughing when I remembered what mi Dad had said " If anyone attacks you and ends up sitting on your face bite his behind" When I carried out mi Dad'ds instructions our John squealed and ran out of the bedroom. He came back a few minutes later to inform me that "You've made my bottom bleed!"

The Wireless
(From "Our Pete")

We always had a radio in the back kitchen and it was almost always on. Every Saturday, Sports Report came on and everybody had to be quiet – really quiet because mi Dad had to take down all the football scores so that he could work out who had won St Sebastian's weekly football pools. He would then go somewhere (maybe the Priory that was attached to Seb's church) and mi Dad and some other men would work out all the calculations and draw up a list of who had won, how much they had won and prepare their winnings envelope.

    I remember a real epiphany moment for me. It happened when I was 3,4,or 5 yrs old. The memory is very clear but my age at the time is not. There was a man singing on the radio and mi Dad joined in. It sounded really good, magical even, to me when mi Dad joined in but he wasn't singing the same as the man on the radio. This was like a thunderbolt to me and had a massive impact on the rest of my life as it was my introduction to harmony.

Mi Dad and the Over Heated Kitchen

As soon as the weather became much cooler my favourite place at "47" was in the rocking chair in the kitchen. I am talking about the time of the year when it is too cold to sit in other rooms where there is no heating but there was always a fire in the back kitchen so I tried my best to grab the rocking chair and dream away my time; I also used to play my guitar whilst sitting on that chair. Anyway, we always used to watch the clock in anticipation of mi Dad coming home from work. Mi Dad worked about five miles away from home in Pollard Street, Ancoats, Manchester. I am always impressed when I remember that mi Dad used to cycle from home to work and back until he was maybe 60 years plus. Because our house was at the top of a hill it must have needed a fair bit of effort right at the end of his journey home. Because he had to cycle up the hill it must have tired him out and made him pretty warm. So when he came through the front door, parked his bike and walked into the kitchen he always commented on how hot it was in the kitchen, too hot by far, according to mi Dad. He immediately opened the door from the kitchen to the lobby (which was cold – no heating there) then the door into the outhouse/shelter (even colder) and made us all shiver. Ten minutes later when he had cooled down from his exertions on the bike he would stand up and say, "That's better, you can shut them doors now".

~ Narrator's Note~

Although this book was Joe's idea he didn't write his contributions down, and Gerard, Tom, and Neville didn't get the opportunity. While they are all mentioned in one place or another I thought I would do a little screed on each of them, so here goes:

REMINISCENSES

Joe
(From Anthony)

Joe was a talented artist who was taught by, and was a friend of Harold Riley. Joe & Pete who performed as "Me and Our Kid" played for Harold at an exhibition of his Manchester United paintings. (As an aside Harold was a junior at Manchester United and became a great friend of Matt Busby who gave him permission to sit at the side of the field with his easel. You will see samples of Joe's work throughout this book as some of his drawings of "4"7 will be included. He worked for the City of Salford and at the time of his death was their longest serving employee. He was very well respected and there are plaques mentioning him in several places (one is in Fire Station Square directly behind the Fire Station). Another plaque is in Roe Green Worsley. He was also a Governor at St Boniface school. He was very involved in the Totem Pole project, and indeed I think he started it (I remember when he wrote me...cause I live on the West coast of Canada, to try to get information on a carver who comes from this area). Just remembered something else. At school Joe made a lute, and the box he made for it looked somewhat like a coffin, so of course he put a plate on the box which read "Here lies Lute"!

(From Pete)

I had been playing guitar for quite a while and had borrowed a banjo from a friend. Angela and me had become pretty close and had begun singing songs in harmony. I think the first song we sang together was probably Stewball. Maybe because he heard us two singing he fancied joining in because all of a sudden our Joe became interested and wanted to learn the banjo. I gave him a quick lesson and he enjoyed himself playing a few tunes. He realized fairly soon that the banjo was a bit limiting so asked me to show him how the guitar worked. It was around this time that we began to spend more time together, the three of us; Joe, Angela and me singing all kinds of music including the three song medley from the film "The Five Pennies". When Joe was 16 he started to play with other lads from school and discovered the joys of finger-picking that I was only just learning. Because Joe was hanging out with friends who were more folky (I had been in a beat group and then singing solo in pubs for four years or so) Joe raced ahead of me in finger-picking and formed a group with some of his friends. I went to see him a couple of times at De La Salle gigs but he moved on to playing at the MSG (Manchester Sports Guild). The MSG had been a popular venue for jazz for years but a folk session began upstairs and flourished attracting top names in folk music including Paul Simon. When Paul Simon appeared there he invited a friend of his up from the audience to join him during the second spot, a feller called Art Garfunkel.

Joe enjoyed his flirtation with folk music which remained with him for the rest of his life, but he also became more and more attracted to pop music, especially Beatles music. As the weeks passed Joe and I spent more time together honing our harmonies and thoroughly enjoying ourselves. I was still singing solo in pubs and clubs and the two of us sang together on family occasions. It became clear that we should become more organized and learn enough songs for us to start working together on stage. We needed a name and I don't know which one of us suggested it but it was never really considered it was "The Martwins". Yea well!!! Anyway fast forward a short time and we found ourselves in a small social club in Langley Road near the UMP for an audition show. This was the type of occasion that Concert Secretaries organized so that different acts would do a short spot and the concert secretaries would arrange to book them for their clubs if they were deemed suitable. The story was that when the compere asked us who was next on, one of us said, "Me & Our Kid" and it stuck. I don't know how true that was but it is such a good story that we just accepted it!

~Another Narrator's note~
After Joe's tragic death there were a couple of books circulating where people had written their memories of Joe. Harold Riley's was a particularly poignant entry and is reproduced here.

I remember a house in Seedley that was really only a part of a row of what had been 12 houses. There was always music coming from that house and it was a happy place — then one day I passed and it was gone. Ralph Steadman 2010.

REMINISCENSES

Gerard
(From Anthony)

Gerard was couple of years older than me, and we were quite close. Random things I remember: At "47" our teapot was a 23 cupper!, and Gerard was the one who got it. His first job was at a place called Berry & Warmingtons, who I think supplied equipment to restaurants, we'd never seen a teapot that big before (or since!). He did his National Service in the navy and during that time he sailed all the way round the British Isles. When he left the forces, like Uncle Eddie & Uncle James he didn't really want to do any more travelling outside of England. He did make 2 exceptions, one was his honeymoon when they went to Austria (I suspect that was Ol's doing), and the other when he came to Canada. Gerard was a good dancer, and of course all the girls fell for him. Many years later when I was at Angela Mather's 21st at the Racecourse, I remember a girl who we grew up with (not telling her name) and from her comments…she still fancied him! I think he had probably turned 60 at that time.

When we were at St Sebastian's school (this was before he won a scholarship so he'd be about 10…making it 1940ish) there had been a lot of burglaries in the area and 2 detectives came to school (one of them was known as "Babyface). They asked Fr Corcoran if he could give them the name of a boy who would be truthful, and of course he gave them Gerard's name. They asked Gerard if he could name anyone who had a lot of keys……………Gerard said "Yes. Our Anthony" So I got called down, had to go home get the keys..of course it was only something I had for playing (maybe a jailer)…That was the last I saw of the keys,..and talking of keys For several years when I visited from Canada I had a deal with Gerard. He would provide me with a bed, and we could eat out at a restaurant at my expense, and we did this, returning to his house in the evening to drink his scotch. However one of the things I noticed was that in his kitchen there was a board with 4 or 5 sets of keys hanging there. It turns out that he was the "key" man in the neighbourhood and when neighbours went on holiday he looked after their home. Seems such a coincidence that after the incident at school so many years ago with the keys, I'd finish up in a Penitentiary (working there!) and he'd be involved with keys.

Tom
(From Anthony)

Tom, unfortunately died long before this book was thought of, hence no submission from Tom. He was a couple of years younger than me, and he was "ahh so meticulous" in everything he did. When he wallpapered he took longer than anyone else but his work was PERFECT. He was thorough. At one time the kitchen floor at 47 was sloping & it was flagstones. The floor was dug up, the ground levelled, some kind of insulation was laid. And then concrete mixed (by hand!) and laid. This was done by my Dad & Tom...a big job.

Tom also had the unique position of choosing his own name! (Which is why 2 successive brothers have the same second name). At the time of his baptism no name had been chosen for him, so his godfather (Joe Murphy) put a bunch of names in a hat, put Tom's hand in the hat and the two names that stuck to his little fingers were Thomas & Edmund.

Joe Murphy's son was born about 6 months after Tom and he was named Joseph Edmund Murphy. The two of them were very close and were known as Tom-Ed & Joe-Ed. When they were very little they talked to one another and nobody could understand them, but they certainly seemed to understand one another.

One other thing I remember about Tom was his willpower! For Lent he gave up chocolate, and you might think "So What?" However he took a bar of chocolate, put it on the mantelpiece in the boys' bedroom and left it there until Easter Sunday. Apart from Tom's willpower, the only other reason it stayed there was because us other lads wouldn't steal from our brother.

I had the idea that we should have a serving hatch between the kitchen and the middle room, but I didn't do it. Tom & my Dad took bricks out of the wall and installed the serving hatch, which was much used.

Neville
(From Anthony)

His full name was George Neville Martin, the Neville bit was after a Canadian cousin of my Mam's who I think was in England at the time Neville was born. Neville had a phenomenal memory (most of the time) and should really have been a tour guide. He also had the world's largest supply of (often corny) jokes. In fact he was so well known for this that one of his children distributed a page of Neville's jokes at his funeral. A cousin of Heather's once visited England and Neville toured him around. When the man came back he gave a talk at his club about the canal at Worsley (the one with red water, think it's the Bridgewater canal). Neville was the best man at our wedding, and liked Canada so much he came back several times.

He was an absolute stickler for punctuality. He was late for work ONCE in his lifetime. It was foggy, he left early and caught the 70 bus by the bus depot, which went to town, along Deansgate and Neville worked somewhere near Knott Mill. He was very frustrated, figured he could get there quicker than the bus and got off near Kendal Milnes! However he was still late, and was still angry when he got home that night!. I often thought that if he arranged to meet a girl at 7.00, he'd be there at 6.45 and if she was a minute late he'd be saying: "Where've you been? I've been waiting here for 15 minutes!

Just after having written the above, I found the eulogy from Neville's funeral, written by my sister Pauline (who did a much better job than I did), so even if there is some repetition here is what Pauline wrote:

My elder sister Mary reminded me of an early memory she has of Neville. He was just a toddler and my mother took him shopping in his pram to Cross Lane market where she bought a pound of cheese which she placed in the pram. On arriving home, there were only a few crumbs of cheese left in the bag. Neville had eaten all of it. That's when he discovered his life long love of Cheshire cheese.

Neville was 7 years my senior and liked to be in charge. Sometimes on a Saturday he would take me to Old Trafford to watch United but he once made the mistake of spending the return bus fare on a half time cup of Bovril and so we had to walk home. I cried all the way. After that he refused to take me to Old Trafford but would still take me to the Cliff to watch the reserves and the youth team. It was thanks to Neville and his love of football that I saw the heroes of the '48 cup final, just as Neville's enthusiasm for theatre meant my brother James saw so many of the great comedians of his age.

He was strong willed and once he'd made up his mind about something that was that. When he was at De La Salle, he loved playing football in the park at lunch times, so he refused to wear long trousers as they got in the way and would be messy if he fell over. He wore short trousers to school every day until he left to start work at the age of 16. He was oblivious to any comments about his trousers. It was the same stubbornness that made him leave the house whenever my brother Tom started to practise the bagpipes. Neville hated them with a vengeance. His own preference was for brass and military bands. He learned to play the drums when he was doing his National Service in the RAF. He was proud too of his name – George Neville Martin (he was named after my mother's cousin, a Christian brother who lived in Canada). Neville belonged to the Society of St. George and always celebrated St George's day by wearing a red rose to go with his ever-present cross of St. George.

Neville like his father, was very fussy about food but he knew what he liked. Once when our parents were away – and he was left in charge – he served up sausages every day. Peter reminded me it's what he often cooked for us on a Saturday. Eventually there was a rebellion and we told him we would eat no more. The next day Neville announced that we were having a change. What was it........ Sort of burgers- made out of sausage meat. But it wasn't sausages!

He had a fantastic memory for detail. He once worked at Fieldings, a company who made door handles. Whenever he spotted one – visiting a friend, going for a walk, even from the top of a bus – he would point it out and give you the name, serial number and finish. He first visited Canada in 1961 to be the best man for his brother Anthony. Anthony tells me that when visiting Canada 20 years later Neville could still remember in detail what he had done on each day of that first trip. His determination to commit things to memory also benefitted my brother James who was given the job of testing Neville on his Latin verbs, and passages from Shakespeare. Even to this day James can recall Neville's homework from the 1950's.

Long before Facebook, social networking and dating sites we had Neville. My sister Margaret and her husband Brian told me they were eternally grateful to him for introducing them to each other. His remarkable memory and zeal for communication meant that he kept in touch with everyone. Each week, reliable as clockwork the phone would ring – a status update – family news came first and then the inevitable "Remember so and so, lived round the corner..well (lately it tended to finish with…they've died)." But what he loved most was telling you good news – no one could have been a more avid collector of the achievements of others. There are many proud parents who will tell you about their own children and grandchildren and Neville did that; he was very proud of them, but Neville also loved to hear and tell of the success of his friends, brothers, sisters, nieces, nephews, cousins, aunts, uncles. Everyone. His joy was spreading good news and happiness.

He was a kind generous man. Generous most especially with his time. Any visitor to the city would be treated to a full, some might say exhaustive, tour of Salford; he was a dedicated church worker offering his services as a drummer, mini bus driver, and administrator; we were all lucky enough to share in his many jokes and plays on words – no one who knew him was left out. If you agreed that you "liked that one", the chances were that within a week an envelope full of similar material would arrive through the post. He was very sociable and loved family parties where his kindness was often directed towards his nephews and nieces who could always be sure that he would tell a joke or two (hundred). In a crowded and competitive field he is a strong contender for the title of great uncle and a faithful and much loved brother.

Pauline

This is what I received from Pauline:

Hello Anthony; we did talk about things to go in your book the last time you were over and I didn't want to duplicate things you already had. Now I can't remember what they were!

Has anybody told you about the milk stealer? It was mostly me. Late at night when we came in and wanted coffee and there wasn't any milk, I was good at finding the bottle my Dad had hidden to make sure he had some for breakfast and to take some to work in his old medicine bottle. I was also adept at stroking the metal top just enough to lift it off. I took enough milk for coffee and then filled up the bottle with water. I carefully replaced the tin foil top and hey presto all was well, until years later when somebody (naming no names but maybe James) told on me....my Dad was flabbergasted and reproached me but with a smile and a twinkle in his eye. I think he enjoyed the story especially as he felt vindicated about the claims he made at the time about watery milk, which had been pooh poohed.

Did anyone tell you about the diary my Dad was given at a co-op function? He brought it home and lo and behold unbeknown to him, there were some perforated stickers inside to be put in to mark significant days. So when he opened the diary a few days later he was beside himself with amazement because "tomorrow is my wife's birthday, tomorrow is my wedding anniversary" stickers were in exactly the right place. He was ready to write to the publishers, write to the co-op, the Reporter etc. He was so enthused about what he was going to do that we couldn't contain our mirth, eventually we exploded with laughter. He got the joke too.... eventually.

When I was still going to tap dancing classes and was showing off how I could kick above my height, my Dad said he could do that. He got up made an almighty swing with his leg and...unfortunately caught his toe under the arm of the armchair, he lifted it off the floor. Guess who was sitting in it? Oh my, he just said in strained tones,"get to bed the lot of you"...it must have hurt a lot.

When we came back from Canada and were living in Chippenham I phoned home for a catch up. Unusually my Dad answered the phone and he was in a bit of a state. He told me how he had bought some brushes to clean the chimney. As I understand it the brush could be extended by screwing on extra handles. He had done this in the middle room and everything was going well until he tried to get the brush down. One of the extensions came off and the brush was poking out of the top of the chimney. He couldn't get it out but eventually he got our Joe to go up the chimney and sort it out on the promise of extra spends if he succeeded. I was laughing so much at his description I nearly wet myself.

Did you hear about the first time he papered the kitchen ceiling. Tom was helping and there were quite a few of us watching. He put two sets of ladders at opposite ends of the kitchen with a plank of wood between them. Tom measured the paper and put the paste on and handed it to my Dad who was on the plank. Tom also held up the long handled kitchen brush with a cloth over the brush. The idea was that my Dad would hold the wallpaper and unfold it onto the ceiling. It was so comical, the brush went straight through the paper which stuck to my Dad and fell all about the place. We didn't wait for "Get to bed the lot of you" we just went quick as we could. But I'm telling you it was pure farce. All that after a hard day at work!

John
(From "Our John")

Story 1

My summer holidays.
    Anthony was the only one with the bad habit of smoking.
    But we didn't know it was a bad habit, we thought it was big and clever to smoke.
    Me, being always very kind and thoughtful offered up 2 days of my school holidays (about 1956-57) to walk the streets of Salford picking up dimps (butt end of a cigarette), When I had a full tin of dimps I emptied the tobacco into a tin to save our Anthony having to buy cigarettes. When I presented the tin of bacca to my big brother, expecting a big thank you for my efforts, Instead I was met with a very short silence whilst he examined the contents THEN a dual action of a very loud

shout, (I was stood next to him, I could have heard a whisper) and a clout across the back of my head.

To this day I have NEVER collected any more dimps.

Story 2

Pete and I had a zoo in the shelter and the back yard. At the time the old bath was in the back yard, Pete and I had a walk to Drinkwater Park to catch some fish for the bath (sticklebacks and something else). We also had 21 rabbits and 2 Guinnea pigs in the yard a couple of caterpillars and 2 spiders. To add to our zoo Pete and I walked down to Pet's corner to buy a white mouse.

I asked the man "how much are your mice" one and six came the reply. O I said (only having a shilling) can I have a gold fish instead, they were only 9 pence.

We also brought back some frogs from Drinkwater Park, we put them in the front garden with a bowl of water, and there was also 2 tortoise that shared the garden with the frogs. Unfortunately the frogs ended up down the grid in the cellar mixed with the coal. We know this because on one occasion that Pete went to get some coal, he came back up the cellar steps twice as fast as he went down complaining that the coal was jumping at him. That's when we found the frogs.

Story 3

I spent a lot of my childhood across the road in Harry Marshall's garage. One day he was spraying a grey undercoat of paint on a car. Marshall being Marshall tested the paint on a brick he gave me the brick and told me to look after it. Keep it clean and don't let it get wet.

That brick ended up under my pillow for quite a few nights.

Story 4

Being one of the young ones we had the hand me downs. I had a problem coming after our Pauline. One time having to wear her white buckled sandals for school. I painted them with blue ink the night before (they didn't look good and for those few days I didn't play out).

Story 4A

I was the last in line to take possession of our Mary's bike (what was left of it)

There was more spokes missing from the front wheel than on the wheel. I took the bike over to Marshall's garage to ask Bert to repair it. Now Bert was Harry Marshall's Helper. He believed there was only two things in the world, a "doings" and a "whatsit". Oh and also a "touse".

Bert was unable to find any spokes the correct size and that was the end of Mary's bike.

There was a damaged car in the garage at the time waiting for someone to pick it up (I think it was someone called Cookie). Bert said if you can get the car in your house before Cookie comes you can have it. I have never been so excited, forget our Mary's bike I've got a car. If my Mam would let me put it in the house. And she said you had best hurry up before Cookie come. Cookie came before I got MY car in, the trouble was the front door wasn't wide enough.

Story 5

I had forgotten about this but our Joe reminded me about it.

He (Joe) was working at Belle Vue fairground and one bank holiday Monday was only paid single time for his shift. Obviously he was upset. So for my little brother I phoned his boss. I think his name was Mr Lion. On the phone I was Joe's Dad and I worked for the Inland Revenue.

I suggested that Mr Lion checks Joes pay slip and correct the short fall payment before I make a call to his place of work. Joe got his money and never got paid short again.

Story 6

I remember the time I bought a white mouse without my Mam knowing. I kept the mouse in a shoe box under my bed, until our Anthony came home. He heard something squeaking and found the box and the mouse nibbling a hole in the box. He took the box down stairs.

The mouse escaped but we found it 2 days later when we heard Mrs Marshall shout there's a mouse in the kitchen. So I helped her get rid of the mouse. (Wasn't I good?)

Story 7

Cleaning the rabbit hutches.

We had 3 hutches on top of each other in the back yard. Occasionally Anthony would clean them out, He would scrape all the muck out change the straw and wash the floor with St Izal disinfection. Then the scientific stuff. He would light 2 or 3 candles and put them inside the hutches to dry them out. I was never very good at science (or school for that matter) but I knew that 2 candles burning outside in the yard would NEVER dry out the hutches. But I wasn't brave or daft enough to tell our Anthony.

Story 8

New Year's Eve.

Pete, Joe and I were not allowed to stay up for the New Year, I rebelled and said to our Pete, I am not getting in bed till next year, at the time our James had an electric clock (very rare in the 50's) with no plug on. On the wall next to James' bed he had a lamp holder for the alarm bell that my Dad rang for our James to get up for work. So I had the idea to test this electric clock. I push the two bare wires into the live lamp holder and out came a big blue flash. Before the flash had gone out I was in bed. Never touched the clock again, James, honest.

Story 9

Whilst the front gutter was being repaired all the boys had to sleep in the front room. One Saturday when Neville was having a lie in someone took our Angela's big black doll and laid it next to him in bed. Then we made enough noise to wake Neville up. He was normally pretty fast at getting up but never as fast as on that occasion.

TALES OF FORTY-SEVEN

Mary
(From Anthony)

Mary is mentioned several times by her siblings, so in her case I will simply print some of her poems. Many incidents were commemorated by her in verse, but most relate to her life in Canada. Some of them were published on Facebook in the "Salford" scene. Herein are the poems.

The poem on page 83 was written on the occasion of Anthony's 80th birthday, and the one on the next page was about mi Mam when she was in Canada & won a prize at the Ag Rec fair in Abbotsford.

REMINISCENSES

Poem written 24 Sept 2013 by Mary Dereume

Eighty years ago today
My mother in despair
Gazed upon the baby
Dod submitted to her care
Indeed she wondered how to cope
It seemed as though there was no hope

For this babe who looked so wierd
A problem child, for sure, she feared
Along came Mary, four years old
Her words of truth left mother cold.

He looks like a monkey, Mary cried
This observation could not be denied,
By anyone, specially my mother
Since Mary's reaction to her brother
Was to the point, precise and true
And left Mam wondering what to do
With this scrap of human kind
Shades of Darwin crossed her mind

She did her best, and through the years
Was often found in floods of tears
Wondering why she had to suffer
The trouble caused by this little duffer
Years rolled on, and he grew older,
And was accepted as a soldier,
Later on, Canada quite desperate
Took a chance on this expatriate.

Then along came Heather, full of beans
Fortified by ways and means
Of knowing how to get her man,
Skating was her Master plan

Blinded by true love, he fell
Hook, line and sinker under her spell
So they were wed one day in June
So now I'd like to make a toast
To a guy who is known from coast to coast
As King Kong's double for ever after
(accompanied by hearty laughter)

TALES OF FORTY-SEVEN

Settle down and listen, whilst I tell to you a tale
Of the natty little knitter, who lives on Overdale.
She sits there busily knitting, morning, noon and night,
Producing lots of dollies, in colours warm and bright.
Chimney-sweeps and scarecrows, bees and doggies, too
All you do is ask her, and she'll make one just for you.
For years and years, she's knitted toys and dollies by the score.
You'd think that she'd get tired, but no, she.s busy knitting more.
Children and great grandchildren, friends and neighbours too
Own toys from her woollen family, which grew and grew and grew.
At last, her talent recognised at the Fraser Valley Fair,

She came out a winner of Blue Ribbons, (by the pair)
But those needles keep on clicking, making hats and scarves and shoes
Bagpipes, kilts and haggis, not forgetting trews.

REMINISCENSES

Margaret
(From Anthony)

Margaret was quiet and unassuming (well most of the time). She was an accomplished pianist (as were Mary, Pauline & Angela), and very, very, good on a sewing machine. She made most if not all of her children's clothes, as well as much of Brian's. She also made Emma's wedding outfit & probably many things I don't know about. I remember I once took her to the Ice Palace on Derby St and when I introduced her as my sister they didn't believe me, thinking it was a new girl-friend.

James
(From "Our James")

The earliest recollection I have in my life, was being carried down the cellar steps at "47" by our Gerard when the sirens had sounded for an air raid. The plan was that the older children were each assigned a younger brother or sister to take them to the safety of the cellar. Other early memories include coming down on Christmas morning to inspect our present. I can still recall the smell of new paint on my present although I can't remember what it was and being told that the elves finished it just in time to be delivered. It was only years later that I realized it was my Dad that had made the toy.

The kitchen at "47" was the hub of the house as it was the kitchen/living room. Our Mary was quite an artist I remember being told to sit on a stool near the open fire with my foot on the coal scuttle while Mary drew a sketch of me.

Mary was working at this time at Co-operative head office in Balloon St. Manchester. When she got paid she would bring home a quarter pound box of Cadbury's chocolates and give us one each. You must remember that chocolates were on ration and this was a real treat.

In the kitchen we had what was called a Bungalow Range fireplace which consisted of an opening at the side of the fire where there was a steel plate(called a damper) which could be adjusted to allow the heat from the fire to heat the oven. (there was a similar damper at the back of the fireplace to allow the water to be heated) The oven part was not used very often after we got an electric oven but I seem to recall that it was used at Christmas as the electric oven wasn't big enough for the turkeys. Talking about turkeys, I remember my Dad coming home from work with a huge turkey which I think he bought at Smithfield market. Not only was it huge but it still had all its feathers on! We had some fun when we were told to pluck all the feathers off!

There was an issue with the coal fire in as much that when the fire died down more coal was required and this had to be brought up from the cellar. A call would go out saying that "the fire wants some coal on" this would be followed with "its not my turn, I went last" and other such comments.

The coal was delivered by horse and cart at that time and we often fed a crust to the horse. In the summer coal was cheaper, so my Dad bought a ton of coal (that' twenty bags) with the dividend from the co-op, and it would be tipped down the manhole outside the front door. More often than not, I our John and Peter would have to go down the cellar and rake the coal away from the manhole so that all the coal could be tipped down.

The cellar was where my Mam used to do the washing, no washing machines in those days. In the corner of the cellar was a copper boiler, you had to light a fire under the boiler to heat the water that was in the boiler. The washing was put in the hot water, then taken from the boiler and put into a dolly tub which was full of cold water, the washing then had to be pummelled with a posher. A posher was a broom handle with a piece of copper on the end, shaped like half a football which was full of holes. The clothes then had to be taken out of the tub and put through the wringer which had to be turned by hand. The pummelling and the wringing was a job for us when available. What a change from all the singing and dancing washing machines of today.

In the summer holidays we generally had to make our own entertainment. There were quite a few children of our age living in the nearby streets, we would often play cricket in London Street, with the bottom of the gas lamp post as the wickets. The gas lamp was outside the side of the house which we used to call the "back wall". Occasionally the adults would join in i.e. my Dad and our next door neighbour Harry Marshall. On the side of the house near to Broughton Road was fixed the street sign for London Street. This section of the wall which was part of the front room, was used for a number of things. One game was to hit each letter of the London Street sign in order with a tennis ball. There was also a sign painted on the wall which was to do with the war (it was a sign indicating where the nearest emergency water supply was for fire-fighters), again we used to try and hit the letters in the sign with the ball. The wall was also used by the girls for playing two ball and hand stands. London Street was made of cobble stones and this was ideal for playing "allies" otherwise known as marbles. London Street was also good for playing rounders, although this didn't always go down well with Molly Sloan, Molly was a spinster who lived in the house on the other side of London Street. I remember once when she told us to stop playing ball we decided to carry on playing, but not use the ball, but pretended to be playing with one. When she told us to stop playing with the ball, we told her that we didn't have one. Drawing numbers on the paving stones to play hop scotch was another game. Hide and seek was yet another favourite, apart from running through the back entries which sometimes stunk to high heaven. We managed very well without TV, computers, and all the other electronic paraphernalia.

We did see some interesting sights such as the lamplighter who came at night to turn on the gas light near the back wall. The knocker up, who some people paid to wake them up in the morning. To carry out this task he had a long pole with bits of wire attached to the end, he would tap the bedroom windows with the wires at the end of the pole. No alarm clock in those days. Then there was a street singer who had two walking sticks and would walk down the middle of the side streets singing, he had a tin around his neck for people to put money in. Occasionally there was a man who would come round with a barrel organ, he would stop outside the Wellington Inn and wind the handle to make music. There was also a man who came on a push bike which had been adapted so he could sharpen knives for a fee.

I mentioned the "Wellington Inn". Us lads used to sleep in the front bedroom which had sash windows. In the summer we always had the windows wide open.

The Wellington had a piano and at weekends somebody would play the piano for a sing-along, and it goes without saying that we joined in. When the pubs closed, we would be in bed with the lights out. The people would come out and start to walk home and we would shout "Goodnight". They would say goodnight, turn around and see nobody there! Sometimes we would say goodnight a couple of times but they could not make out who was saying it.

There was a cinema on Cromwell Road which was at the bottom of London Street, when the film was over a number of people would walk up London Street and turn left onto Broughton Road and walk past our house. I blame our Pauline for instigating the next part of this story as I never did anything wrong. If you fold a piece of A4 paper a certain way and blow into a small opening at the top, the paper is roughly in the shape of a ball. If you then held it under the tap it would hold water for a short period of time. By looking out of the window in the bathroom and people were walking past the corner of the back of the house, you could work out how long it would take them to reach the front of the house. The sash window in the boy's bedroom at the front of the house would be wide open and it would be possible to fill the ball or waterbomb with water, run along the landing to the window and lob the water bomb toward the person or persons passing by. This would be done on dark nights with the lights off so they had no idea where this water had come from.

In the summer holidays when we together with the other kids from the neighbourhood on the front, it was quite common for Noonan's ice cream cart to come round and if Harry Marshall was in the garage he would treat all the kids to an ice cream.

I remember once in the winter when we had a good fall of snow and our Anthony and Harry Marshall were having a snowball fight.

Our Anthony caught Harry Marshall right on the back of the neck with a snowball. We then saw Harry Marshall pick up a snowball; Our Anthony ran into the house, down the lobby, through the kitchen and into the back yard with Harry Marshall chasing him every step of the way. (James doesn't mention that Harry did catch me and then him and Bert rolled me in the snow!)

In the Autumn we would keep an eye on Marshall's garage to see what cars he would buy. We were not interested in the cars but waiting for an ex-army lorry to arrive. This would signal a forthcoming trip to Blackpool. Harry Marshall would install supports at the back of the cab which he would cover with a tarpaulin sheet. The date would be agreed and then on the night the back of the truck would be filled with us and some local kids and we would be driven to Blackpool to see the Illuminations.

(You may not realise that at this time petrol was rationed, and commercial vehicles had to use coloured (red) petrol and there were penalties involved if red petrol was used for pleasure trips. Harry, therefore arranged for a friend to drive to Blackpool, have a" breakdown" and wait in a certain spot for Harry, who would then (supposedly) fix the problem & the man could drive home – the man was a chap that worked at the dog track as a tic-tac man)

I will never forget the morning during the school holidays when we had not yet got dressed and were larking around. I was stepping from one bed to another when our John gave me a push in the back. This push came just as I was moving my weight from the back foot to the front foot; this made my foot miss the bed. My shin hit the angle iron which was part of the frame of the bed. I remember thinking I must have a big bruise on my shin, should I chase our John and then look at the bruise, or look at the bruise first. I decided to look at the bruise; I pulled up my pyjama trousers and let out a blood-curdling scream. My shin had scraped down the angle iron and the flesh on my leg was rolled up like a Swiss roll exposing over an inch of my shin bone. I went down the stairs, as soon as my Mam saw it she sent someone to Mrs Sharp to phone for an ambulance. I ended up in the ambulance and being taken to the old Salford Royal Hospital with the alarm bell ringing and having twenty stitches put in the wound.

There was another incident I witnessed but it was not at "47." I think that I had been taken to the Doctors on Blackfriars street by my Mam. I remember when we were walking past some shops when my Mam let out a funny cry. It appeared that the elastic in her knickers had snapped and her knickers were now around her ankles! My Mam swiftly stepped out of her knickers and carried them into one of the shops where urgent repairs were carried out.

In the back yard we used to keep rabbits and sometimes guinea pigs. My Dad made the rabbit hutches originally and they lasted for some time, but eventually they had to be repaired or new ones built. The hutches sat one on top of the other and were situated against the kitchen wall at the back of the fireplace so that in the winter they would get some benefit from the heat of the fire. The rabbits were mainly Dutch but we did have an English rabbit which was mainly white with black spots on its spine, this rabbit was called Charlie. The rabbits would very often be let out of the hutches and given the freedom of the back yard. Although this was good enough for most of the rabbits it was not good enough for Charlie. Charlie would run up the steps and into the kitchen and lie down on the mat in front of the fire. We did keep the buck and doe in separate cages, but occasionally they managed to meet up with each and hey bingo, guess what!! At one time I think there were ten rabbits running round the yard. I seem to remember that I did most of the cleaning out of the hutches and going to shops to beg for fresh straw.

In Memoriam.

It is with deep regret that we must inform you of the passing away of our beloved pet rabbit

"Charlie"

Who passed away
On Christmas day
That memorable date,
At the age of eight,
Of his body we're loth
To make "Rabbit Broth"
So now we'll inter,
What we once called a pest
Where he will not stir
In a garden of rest

Author AEMartin

REMINISCENSES

I had a school pal named Alan Rowlett who lived in the house in Walsall Street where we used to live. Alan would come quite often to our house. our Joe was only young and Alan gave Joe a matchbox with rabbit droppings in and told him they were rabbit eggs.Joe kept that box for ages.

I remember one time when our Anthony came home and he didn't have his door key, I must have been out with him I can't remember why, but the situation was that we were locked out. Our Anthony the lifted the grid where the coal was tipped, and made me climb down the grid to gain access to the cellar, climb up the cellar steps and then open the front door.

Things happened at "47" which we accepted without question. One day our Pauline turned up with three French boys. Pauline was somewhere on Cross Lane near to Broad street when the boys stopped her and asked if she knew where there was a field where they could pitch their tents. Without hesitation Pauline told them that they could stay at "47". When they arrived my Mam said that they could sleep in the front room in their sleeping bags. I think they stayed for three nights.

When we were young my Dad had an allotment on Littleton road. At weekends he would often take us with him, it must have been those trips that made me interested in gardening. There was a shed on the allotment which when you opened the door had that nice earthy smell. My Dad would give us jobs to do like weeding, turning the soil over, digging up potatoes etc. We had a patch of rhubarb which we used to pick and sometimes eat raw. There was a man who had the next plot who my Dad would often talk to that was until the man was arrested for murder.

In the front room we had a piano which was used quite often, My Mam ,Mary, Tom, Peter, Joe, Angela and occasionally my Dad, but only on the black keys. I can remember when my Mam used to play and sing, one of her favourites was I'm called little Buttercup from Gilbert & Sullivan's Pinafore. There was a pile of music and I used to build imaginary pictures in my mind from the titles, Pirates of Penzance, Walk across the desert, March of the tin soldiers. Our Tom taught me to accompany him playing chopsticks which I really enjoyed.

The piano we had was an old upright which had seen better days and because the piano was well used and past its sell by date so my Dad decided to buy a new one, we were now a two piano family.

This was the time when Winifred Atwell was all the rage with her Honkey Tonk piano, so our Tom not wanting to be outdone, took the front off the piano and put a drawing pin on the head of every hammer so that when the key was pressed the head of the drawing pin would hit the piano strings thus giving off a tinny sound.

One eventful night was when George and Eddie Garner came round to our house to have a sing song. George and Eddie sang a few duets including the memorable Bold Gendarmes. We did quite a lot of singing that night, but a big surprise was when my Dad started to sing. Part of this evening including my Dad's singing was caught on a tape recorder. My Dad had quite a nice tenor voice.

There was the time when Harry Marshall asked my Mam if he could store some car batteries in the cellar. I am not too sure of the details but I seem to recall that from time to time a man would call to take one away, I think this happened until the last one had gone. I seem to recall a suggestion that the batteries were dodgy.

When I started work my Dad would shout telling me it was time to get up for work. I frequently failed to hear him and consequently he would get annoyed. This went on until I decided enough was enough and so I installed a bell at the side of my bed and put a bell push at the side of my Dad's bed.

When it was time for me to get up my Dad would ring the bell. When the bell was rung I would shout to my Dad that I was awake. Now the boot was on the other foot as my Dad did not always hear me and kept on ringing the bell. I solved the problem by putting a switch at the side of my bed so that when the bell rang, I could switch it off.

I remember one Summer day when we had a visit from an American soldier, I don't know how he came to be at "47" but I do recall our Gerard putting his uniform on and parading outside the house in it.

Our Tom once bought a car off Harry Marshall it cost all of £5. Tom was very careful and was surprised when the car ran out of petrol, complaining that he should have been able to travel another three miles before having to put petrol in.

Our Tom was very meticulous in all that he did, when he did was wallpapering, every piece had to be measured, it took him ages, but it was good when it was finished. At the time there was an advert on television for Murray mints, the too good to hurry mints, somebody, I think it was our Neville gave him the nickname of Murray Mint.

Gerard, James, Anthony, Tom, Neville, John and Joe mimicking George & Eddie Garner. 1978

Part II of the Epistle according to James
(From "Our James")

When our John was young he used to talk to (pester) Harry Marshall. One day Harry Marshall was spraying a car when John asked what he was doing. Having explained to John that he was spraying a car, he then spied half a brick that was nearby, sprayed it grey and then gave it to John. From then on John took the brick everywhere with him wherever he went (even to bed),

Every Thursday night the lads went down to church for choir practice with the men in the choir listening to them when they practised their individual parts. We would walk home past the chipshop on Gerald Road. I seem to remember that it was possible to obtain scratchings (bits of batter from the fish) but I don't know if we had to pay for them.

When we arrived home it was time to go to bed, we would lie in bed and start to sing again what we had been singing in the choir, but this time we would mimic the way that the men in the choir had been singing.

Talking about singing reminds me of a time at Christmas when Fr Matthew Rigney gathered members of "The Children of Mary" and took them round the parish singing carols. They came to "47"; the younger ones were in bed by this time. The choristers sang a few carols and then Fr Matthew and I think some of the singers came upstairs. One of the singers was Sheila O'Brien who years later became my sister-in-law.

I remember when Anthony used to go ice skating and in particular when he went to a fancy dress. He decided to go as a skeleton. He had some old black trousers and a black top onto which he painted bones with white paint and then covered his face with flour and black cork around his eyes and mouth. He had arranged to be picked up by one of his pals so got himself dressed up while some of us were on the lookout for his pal's car. It was a dark night, somebody spotted a car coming down Broughton Road with his headlights on, Anthony then went and stood in the middle of the road waving his arms. The car started to swerve all over the road and as it got nearer Anthony realised it was NOT his pal.

There was a time at "47" when we had a problem in the boy's bedroom and we had to have the bedroom replastered. this caused major problems which involved moving the beds from the bedroom to the front room downstairs. I was in a bed directly beside the window, there was a window sill running underneath the windows. On the window sill we had a bowl which had some frog spawn in it which had matured into tadpoles. I remember waking up one morning with black marks all over my arm. I realised that during the night I must have knocked the bowl over and the black marks on my arm were in fact dead tadpoles. (This must have been the same incident Pete described!).

The only toilet we had at "47" was in the back yard. To access the toilet you had to go out of the back door, go round past the shelter and into the toilet. There was no light in the yard or the toilet, so if you had to pay a visit it could be a bit of a challenge particularly if it was raining. One night I went out to the toilet, went to sit down and heard a big scream. I hadn't noticed our Mary was already sitting there!

Opposite Grandad's house which was on Littleton Road (always known as No 1) was the Manchester Racecourse,(why it was called the Manchester Racecourse when it was in the middle of Salford I will never know) On race days we would go upstairs at number one and looking through the window we could see the riders making their way to the starting post, we once saw Sir Gordon Richards. The Manchester (in SALFORD) November Handicap was the big race of the year and alway caused a lot of excitement with crowds of people turning up. There was a famous racing tipster who I remember seeing on a number of occasions. His name was Prince Ras Monolulo, he was supposed to be some sort of

African Prince but I think he made that up. He would walk down Cromwell Road on his way to the race course decked out in his colourful robes, feathers on his head and shouting his well known tipsters cry of "I gotta horse."

One day when we were playing outside the front door there was suddenly a lot of excited noise, it soon became apparent what it was all about, for as we looked down Broughton road in the direction of Frederick road there was a man walking in the road alongside an elephant. It appeared that a circus was appearing somewhere in the area. I think it was Billy Smarts and the elephant belonged to the circus. How and why it came to be walking along Broughton road I just do not know.

In the summer holidays one of the big occasions was a day out to Lyme Park. This must have been quite a planning exercise for my Mam as it involved packing a picnic for five or six of us. We would walkup to Pendleton Church and catch the tram to Manchester and then make our way to Central Station (now the G-Mex centre) and catching a train to Disley. Having arrived at Disley we would then walk to Lyme Park a distance of about half a mile. The park ran a bus which had about four open trailers each with about four rows of seating; we would board the bus which would take us up the winding road to the hall all the time on the lookout for reindeer. Once at the top we would put down a blanket and explore the area before being called together for the picnic. We would then just enjoy the wide open spaces and the fresh country air, climbing some small rocks or playing in the stream. Mam would then call us together to pack up our belongings and then we would proceed to walk all the way to the park gates. I remember on one visit my Mam met the head gardener of the park who just happened to be one of the Rigby family and who was my Mam's cousin.

We then walked back to the railway station and caught the train back to Manchester and then the tram to Pendleton church arriving home tired, but very happy.

TALES OF FORTY-SEVEN

My Working Life
(From "Our James")

I left school at the age of fourteen in the Summer of 1957 and one week later I started work; I didn't really know what I had let myself in for. At school we were given some pamphlets to look at, but nobody really explained anything about different types of employment.

A few weeks before I left school, my Dad had made an appointment with a Mr. Barratt who ran a firm of electrical contractors. This contact had been made by my Dad through the Knights of St. Columba of which my Dad was a member.

The day of the meeting we had to catch a bus into Manchester and then another bus (or it could have been a trolley bus) that took us to Beswick; a district of East Manchester that I didn't know existed. At this time I was under the impression that I was going to be a television engineer.

The place of the meeting was an electrical shop at number 300 Ashton New Road. The shop sold electrical appliances and light fittings etc. the room at the back of the shop acted as the office while what I assume was originally, a kitchen had been converted into a small office for the shop manager. The shop manager was a Mr. Joe Rowland who was Mr. Barratt's brother in law. Joe, as well as being shop manager would allocate the jobs to the electrician's as they arrived in the morning. The rooms above the shop was used for storing materials such as cable and fuse boards.

We met Mr. Barratt who asked a few questions, explaining that I would have to wear overalls and have a few basic tools to start with, a pair of pliers, a terminal screwdriver, a larger screwdriver and a ratchet screwdriver. My hours would be 8.00am until 5.30pm Monday to Friday with a one hour break for dinner and 8.00am until 12.00mid day on Saturday. This was a total of 48hours at eleven and a half pence an hour, that's just less than ten pence in today's money this came to a grand total of two pounds and four pence for a week's work.

I had to get up at 6.30am in the morning, go down Broughton Road and catch the number 70 bus into Victoria bus station, walk up to Stephenson Square and catch the 215/216 trolley bus which dropped me off on the opposite side of the road to the shop. If I was late my time would be deducted from my pay.

When I arrived at the shop I had to go up an entry at the back of the shop to the back door where the electricians reported in. We went into the covered back yard where the door leading into the premises had been made into a stable door, it was at this door where the electricians were given their instructions for the day and sent on their way. The staff at the time consisted of six electricians and four apprentices. The first day I was sent upstairs to the store rooms to familiarise myself with the materials we would use.

The first job I went on was to a property not far from the shop. The area was mainly terraced housing, two up, two down and a little kitchen. I was with an electrician called Charlie and our job was to install electric in the house for the first time. We would install four 1-way lights, one 2-way light and one 15amp socket. The total cost for the installation was £48.00, a deposit would be paid of twelve shillings and sixpence (75p) and the rest would be paid weekly at I think five shillings. Not far from the shop was the Bradford Pit (coal mine) consequently a lot miners lived in the terraced houses, the majority of which had coal fires. When installing the wiring for the upstairs lights we needed to gain access to the roof space which, more often than not had no hatch. We therefore had to cut a hole in the lathe and plaster ceiling large enough for me to crawl into. When the hole was nearly complete I had to hold a dustbin lid under the area of ceiling being removed and catch the lathes and plaster before it fell to the floor. I would then have to crawl into the roof space and feed the cables to the new light points. As you can imagine after the years of coal fires the roof was full of soot. When I came out of the roof, I would have to go outside, remove my overalls and give them a good shake. I would often go home looking like the ace of spades as there were no facilities for getting washed, and then travel home on the bus. I don't think that other passengers were very pleased.

Depending on what jobs the electricians were on and whether they needed a lift, determined where we were sent each day. The type of work was varied, it could be in a "rag trade" workshop which would have rows of sewing machines operated by machinists. Each row of machines was run off one electric motor at the end of the row and if one motor was faulty it meant that production on that row was halted. It was essential that the repair was carried out as soon as possible.

As I slowly gained knowledge I would be sent on minor repairs on my own. I was once sent to St. Augustine's presbytery in All Saint's Manchester to repair an electric kettle. Little did I realise that I would strike up a friendship that is still alive to this day. I was met at the presbytery door by Fr. Kevin O'Connor who I did not find out until many years later had a arrived that day to take up his post as curate to Cannon Bernard McKernan. He had previously been on the teaching staff at St. Bede's school. I will recall other meetings with Fr. O'Connor later on.

While working at the shop one Saturday I was sent by Mr. Barratt to four or five properties to collect outstanding monies from customers. The amounts as far as I can remember were in the region of two or three pounds. It seemed easy work but I was quite surprised when at the end of the day I was presented with two shillings and sixpence (twelve and a half pence) for each pound I collected.

Education
(From "Our James")

In my first year at work I had to go to night school three nights a week. The course was at Halton Bank School and one of the teachers was Mr. O'Neil who I would meet again years later when he was headmaster at St. Johns school at Bromley Cross. I was now working five and a half days a week, plus three nights a week night school which didn't leave much time for anything else. The following year I was allowed to go to Salford Technical College, for one day a week plus one night.

The course which I and a number of other lads had been put on at Salford, because there was not at this time an electrical installation course, was an electrical engineering course, which proved to be hard going. When we received our results a number of us failed but were sent to Stretford Technical College as Salford did not have the correct course.

We were only a couple of weeks into the course when the maths teacher became aware that some of us were not up to scratch, but if he had made it known to the college the class would have to close because of the small number that would be left. The teacher told us to keep our mouths shut and he would help us as much as he could.

At the end of the term we were to sit for the City & Guilds "C" certificate and we were given the chance to re-sit the City & Guilds "B" certificate. We were then asked if we wanted to sit the City and Guilds "A" certificate. We said we were sitting the other two so we may as well sit that one as well. I am pleased to say that I passed all three.

J & F Brookes
(From "Our James")

There was a customer of Barratt's called J. & F. Brookes, they were manufactures of furniture and had bought new premises as they had out grown their present ones. The premise consisted of a single story factory that had been empty for some time. Power supplies were needed for the wood cutting machines and drilling machines etc. There were about four of us working there and I was given the job of getting the existing lights working and wiring additional ones where required. There were about four big workshops each carrying out a different operation. There was a problem that the firm's management came across when one of the bosses needed to be contacted. There would be one little office in each area with a telephone, but the sound of a telephone could not be heard above the sounds of the wood cutting machines and the general cacophony of noise. To resolve this I installed a block of four lamp holders in each workshop on a board, each lamp holder had a different coloured lamp. Each manager had a personal colour and as his code was lit he would contact the office. Mobile phones had not yet been invented.

When the bulk of the work was finished I remained at the factory finishing off the bits and pieces plus some extra work which was requested. The owners of the firm were two brothers and were referred to as Mr. Jack and Mr. Fred (Brookes) who I got on with quite well. Later on I was able to buy some bedroom furniture from them at a good discount. When I was a boy at home I received a BAYKO building set which was increased in size over a number Christmases with additional sets. Keeping all the kit together was a problem so I asked one of the bosses if they would make me a box, he said he said," tell me what size you want and I will get it made." The box was made with dovetail joints and is still as strong today.

Belle Vue
(from "Our James")

The firm had a contact at Belle Vue in Ardwick, home of the amusement park, circus and dance halls. To me this was fantastic as every year when children we would be taken on a trip to see the circus, this was one of the highlights of the year and here I was getting paid to be there. The builders had put extensions on the front of the Kings Hall which is where the circus performed. One day I was in the area near to the entrance to the circus ring when George Lockhart, the ringmaster, walked past smoking his ever present big cigar, the elephants were nearby being made ready to enter the ring. At lunch times we would eat our sandwiches and walk round the gardens looking at the animals. One day as we were walking round an animal keeper came and told everyone to get inside a building as a ring tailed lemur had escaped from its cage. We went into the monkey house which was nearest which happened to be where the lemur had escaped from and saw where it had pulled the wire netting off the cage away from the wall. I was looking through the window and could see the animal keeper looking up a tree, next thing he took out a rifle and with one shot, hit the lemur which came crashing to the ground; he then picked it up and put it in a sack. I never did find out if he killed it or tranquilised it.

On another day we were working and power had failed to the freezers in the ice cream shop, the power was off for so long that the ice cream and lollies had started to melt, the proprietor said that they would not be able to sell them so if anybody wanted them they could help themselves. I took a box full of ice lollies wrapped in paper. I then had to travel home from Belle Vue on the number 57 bus, our Angela remembers enjoying them. (Not all of them)

On another occasion at Belle Vue we were rewiring the supplies to the distribution boards in the exhibition hall. There was a firm of exhibition contractors throwing in wiring for the exhibition stands. They would straddle a piece of two inch diameter conduit across the timbers supporting the roof, then suspend metal fluorescent fittings from the conduit using bare strainer wire. I was up a ladder about eight feet off the ground feeding new cables into metal trunking which we had installed. I shouted to my colleague who was feeding the cables to me, to hang on while I moved my foot on the ladder. I put one had on the conduit which was supporting the light fittings not realising that the light fittings were not earthed and that the electric was leaking from the fitting, up the strainer wire and onto the conduit where I put my hand. I was now making a full circuit with electric coming into my body on one side, passing through my body to the other side, consequently I was unable to speak or shout as my vocal chords were paralysed. I don't know how but one hand became free, my voice returned and I let out a big shout, I came down the ladder about three steps at a time, just about conscious. When I got to the bottom of the ladder a gentleman came up to me and asked if I knew where the toilet was!!! The foreman came over to me, asked if I was ok and told me go outside and get some fresh air. After ten minutes or so I went back inside and carried on working and I didn't finish work until half past six. When Mr. Barratt found out he wrote a letter to the company who were responsible for installing the exhibition wiring complaining about the standard of their work. Health and safety was not what it is today.

Talking about health and safety, there were no portable scaffolding access towers then and we needed to reach the apex of the exhibition hall roof to install conduit for the lighting. Belle Vue maintenance staff had a wooden telescopic tower. This consisted of three sections of tower fitted one inside the other which was on a wooden base roughly six foot by four foot. (We had not yet gone metric). To raise the platform you had to pull on a rope until the platform had reached the required height. Unfortunately when the tower reached its maximum height we were still not high enough to carry out the work. To resolve this, the Belle Vue joiners made a fourth section which fitted inside the existing third section. When anybody climbed the tower at least two people had to hold the tower to stop it from falling over as the base was now undersize for the extended height of the tower. Today the whole tower would be condemned.

There was a small theatre like building which was added to the front of the Kings Hall which was used for various short entertainments. One show I remember was an illusionist who would stand outside the theatre with a megaphone encouraging the public to pay and go inside. His script was on the lines of "See her defy gravity as she rises on a bed of air". I had to carry out some electrical work on the stage, as I walked behind the curtains at the back of the stage I could see that there was a piece of equipment consisting of a silent electric motor with a three inch piece of metal attached to it. The metal shaped like a squashed letter "S" on edge which came through the curtains where they met. Attached to this piece of metal was a flat piece of metal which was about four foot long and one foot wide, the metal plate would be positioned on a small bed with a drape covering same. The illusionist would then get his assistant to lie on the bed and he would then send her into a trance. He would then press his foot onto a switch on the floor which would activate the motor behind the curtain and the metal plate would then be lifted up with the assistant on it, when it was about four foot off the ground it would stop, he would then pass one hoop over her feet and another one hoop over her head. Due to the "S" shaped metal he was then able to hold both hoops and pass them along the body , two thirds to the left and then two thirds to the right, giving the impression that there was nothing supporting her.

From then on magic of the illusionists lost a lot of its shine.

Beswick Primary School
(From "Our James")

In 1965 I was in charge of the electrical installation of a new primary school being built in Beswick. The building was at the stage where the walls were built but the roof was not yet watertight and there was water everywhere. In what would be the school hall, steps had not yet been built to get from the hall floor onto the stage the only access being by walking up two planks which went from the floor to the stage. I was walking down the planks and as I approached the end of the plank, I received an electric shock in my legs. Cables had been run around the site for temporary supplies to lights and sockets, one cable was run alongside the plank but was trapped between the plank and the floor; as I walked down the wet plank the pressure had cut through the cable which provided an excellent conductor for the electric. This was at a time before it was illegal to have 240 volt supplies on a building site, which proves the need for some health and safety regulations.

Martin Brothers
(From "Our James)

Round about 1960 I was sent with an electrician called Tom Wytch to an engineering firm in Cornbrook, Stretford. The machine shop was huge with an overhead crane which traversed the length of the workshop; this was used to lift huge machine tools to locations in the workshop where they were to be overhauled. The firm would buy second hand machine tools which were used in the manufacturing industry which at the time was quite strong. The machines consisted of all kinds of lathes for turning metal, some as long as twenty feet, various types of pillar drills, planes and others which I cannot remember. These machines would be stripped completely apart and then rebuilt. As the machines were electrically operated it was our job to strip out the original electrics and then install the new electric when the machines had been rebuilt. This could involve installing conduit between the various items i.e. stop/start buttons, limit switches, emergency stop buttons and three phase starters and the three phase motors that ran the machines. When the works had been completed we would have to connect a temporary three phase supply to the machine. What I did not like at Martin Brothers, was the fact that the day was controlled by a hooter. The hooter would sound at 8.00am as a signal to start work, It would go again at the start and finish of morning break, at five minutes before lunch break it would go again giving you five minutes to remove oil and grease from your hands. The similar format would follow for the second part of the day. I enjoyed working in this environment even though you had to put your bag which contained your sandwiches for dinner on a hook to keep it from the rats. I remember my Dad telling us stories about rats at Hamilton's where he worked, he told us that he used to make traps and that he did manage to catch some.

There were two other large engineering firms that we carried out work for, one was John Shaw which was on Adelphi Street in Salford and the other was Francis Shaw in Clayton. I didn't do any work at John Shaw but did on occasions work at Francis Shaw. At the time I worked there, Shaw's were making huge machines which produced tyres for cars. I understood that these machines were part of a contract to be supplied to some eastern country so that they could manufacture their own tyres. The machines had a large control panel full of timers, contacts, limit switches, timers and relays. The wiring of these panels would be done by Shaw's own electricians who had a bonus system and a time to complete the work. When the machines were tested inevitably faults were found on the wiring but because it would affect their bonus, the company electricians would not carry out the work and that is what we did. We would be presented with a big wiring diagram of the control system with indications of the corrections required and rectify them.

Sometimes when the programme was behind schedule some of our electricians would be called in to do the original wiring. The problem was, that they were not part of the bonus scheme. Apparently the scheme had been agreed with the unions and management with the unions saying it took longer to carry out certain tasks than the management were saying. Eventually a compromise was agreed. The only trouble with this was, our electricians were not tied by the agreement and just worked as normal. It did not take long before the company electricians realised that we were working faster than them and that we could upset their bonus system. Jimmy Potter who was working there had his tools locked in the toilets to stop him working and to make sure that he got the message.

By this time I was sent out working on my own, which meant that I had to find my own way, on public transport, carrying my tools together with materials to the locations of the work. Sometimes if there was too much to carry I would be given a lift to the site and left to do the work.

Nazareth House
(From "Our James")

Because I was a catholic and was able to get on with the priests and nuns, it was inevitably me who was sent to jobs at churches, presbytery's, convents and catholic schools.

I recall one job when I was sent to Nazareth House at Prestwich in the Winter. At the time Nazareth House had a pig sty in the grounds complete with pigs. The sow had had a litter of pigs and I had been instructed to install an infra red light in the pig sty above the piglets.

Carmelite Convent
(From "Our James")

I was sent on a number of occasions to the Carmelite convent on Vine Street. Having been to the convent on a number of occasions, the nuns who answered the door bell knew me. The procedure to get into the convent was, ring the doorbell at the double gates which opened onto a courtyard; after a period of time I would hear the sound of wooden clogs walking across the courtyard. The sliding hatch in the gate would be drawn back to reveal the face of a nun who would then open the gate to let me into the yard. The reception party consisted of three nuns, two of which had their faces covered with veils, while the third nun welcomed me. We then set off across the yard with one nun walking in front of me, one nun at my side who was conversing with me and one nun bringing up the rear. As we processed across the yard the nun in front was ringing a hand bell, this was to warn the other nuns that there was a man on the premises and as we approached I could see figures scurrying away or turning to the wall whilst covering their faces. I was taken to the room where the fault was and to where the fuse board was, as I would need to remove a fuse. Just before the nun left me to carry out the work she handed me the small hand bell and instructed me ring it as I walked to and from the area where the fuse board was. I felt like a leper. On another occasion I had to repair the machine that they made the altar breads on which they supplied to churches. It was a machine with a metal bed which was covered with indents of altar breads, the flower mixture was poured onto the metal bed, a metal cover, also with indents was lowered onto the bed, the heat was then switched on only for a short time then the top plate was raised. This then left a sheet of altar breads which was removed from the machine and the altar breads removed from the sheet. Moving forward to the year 1982 the year the pope came to Manchester, I had reason to visit the convent to see the Reverend Mother. I was ushered into the reception room and shown to a chair which was facing a wooden screen. After a short while the screen was removed to expose a steel grill, on the other side of the grill sat the Reverend Mother. When we had completed the reason for the visit, I asked Rev. Mother with this being an enclosed order, if the nuns would be allowed out of the convent to see the pope at Heaton Park. The Rev. Mother replied, saying that they would be allowed out and that they will be at Nazareth House where the pope would be landing in his helicopter. I said, "You will have a good view then". "Oh yes". Rev. Mother replied. "But we would have a good view anyway" she said. "What do you mean", I answered. "Well" she said, "We would do what our sisters in Rome do". "And what is that" I said. "We would take hat pins with us". "Hat pins "I replied, questioningly. "Yes" she answered as she moved her hand foreword in short sharp jabs. "We would soon reach the front".

There was a follow up to this visit the following week. I was working on the podium when a gentleman carrying a large leather bag over his shoulder, approached me and asked if I knew where Vine Street was. Vine street is the street where the Carmelite convent was, so putting two and two together

I asked if he was going to the convent. When he said that he was, I related the story of the hat pins. I then asked why he was going the convent and he told me that he was making a programme for Radio four. I then said that he was not to use the story without the permission of the Reverend Mother. The gentleman told me when the programme would be broadcast. On the day, I tuned in to radio four and heard the Reverend Mother herself relating the story.

For the visit of the Pope all the electrical work in Heaton Park was to be carried out by two electrical contracting firms, Barratt's (who I worked for) and Sadler and Kinsey. The owner of Sadler and Kinsey was Dorothy Sadler who was a relative of uncle Wilf. The work was split between the two companies in case one of them went into liquidation before the work was completed and if so the company would complete the work and I would be responsible for all the work carried out by 'Barratt's.

The park was split into coloured sections, each section would have a toilet block which had to be lit and also the area would be floodlit. A large motor driven generator would be positioned at each area and an electrical distribution board installed on a column, spare fuses would be located at each board, plus an extension ladder to enable access to the board.

On the day of the visit an electrician would be situated in each area adjacent to the distribution board. I was responsible for all of the work carried out by Barratt's and on the day of the visit I would be responsible for the electrics on and under the podium.

For the two weeks leading up to the visit access to the podium area was only allowed if you were the holder of a security pass issued by the police which was issued only after a police check into your background. There were four large towers installed with floodlights to light up the podium area and I had to go to Heaton Park every night for two weeks to switch the floodlights on for security reasons. I asked the electrical consultant if we could install a time clock. He said,"No" because if any lights failed to come on it could lead to a security risk. One night when I switched the lights on, one tower failed to come on. I checked the supplies at the mains position under the podium and discovered that one of the phases had failed on the incoming main cable and had to call out the electricity board. I had a bit of a job convincing him of the address which I gave as The Podium, Heaton Park. They carried out a temporary repair and returned next morning. They located the fault to the main supply cable where one of the scaffolding poles knocked into the ground to form the crowd barriers had gone through the buried cable.

When the podium was being built I had to have a mains room built with a lockable door, this was for a safety reason. When asked how big would I want the room, I told the joiner eight foot square. I knew that I along with all the other electricians would be on duty for twenty four hours and wanted the room big enough to take a camp bed. Just outside the switch room was a stand tap. I made sure that I took with me an electric kettle, sugar, tea and milk plus ample food. I put my head down eventually and went to sleep, only to be woken up by a police woman who asked if she could boil the kettle to make a cup of tea.

To the left of the podium there was an array of tables on which the purpose made pottery chalices containing the altar breads had been placed and sat adjacent to the tables where rows of nuns who would be distributing communion.

Because I was on stand-by to deal with any electrical problem that may have occurred, I was sat on the front row, together with a fireman who was also on stand-by. At the end of the Mass the Pope went to the front of the podium to acknowledge the congregation, the nuns all made a dash to the front. I said to the fireman, "stay here" knowing that when he had finished he would have to come back past us to reach the sacristy. That just left the two of us in a vast space. Sure enough the Pope came back, saw the two of us, stopped and gave us a blessing. Little did I know that some years later I would shake hands with the Pope in the Vatican.

Clifford Turner
(From "Our James")

JohnTurner was the son of Clifford Turner who owned a chain of up market shoe shops in the Manchester and Cheshire area. While Clifford Turner lived in the Lake District, John Turner lived in Hale Barns and ran the business. The shops were in King St. Manchester, Prestwich, Eccles, Stockport, Cheadle, Altrincham, and Wilmslow that I can remember. Every year he would refurbish one shop with the completion finished in time for Easter. More often than not we would have to work overtime to achieve completion, sometimes working until seven o'clock. Mr. John Turner would always visit the shop on the day of completion and would thank the workers and hand out a tip for completing the work. I received a tip of two pounds on more than one occasion, which in those days was a lot of money. I would also have to visit Mr. Turner's house which was in Hale Barns. I had to go to his house one Saturday morning and as I was travelling on public transport, Mr

Turner said he would meet me in Altrincham when I got off the bus and take me to his house. It was the first time I had had a ride in a Jaguar. I was attending to some electrics in the garden when Mr. Turner came out to see how I was getting on. I had some working shoes on which were reaching the end of their life and said to Mr. Turner that I would have to be visiting his shop in King Street. This was said in jest as the price of shoes in his shops, were far too dear for me. He said nothing and went away. When I had finished the job he said to me, "When you go to King street tell them to give you a pair of shoes on my behalf". I went to King Street and selected a pair of "Barkers" which cost over six pounds. Today you would not be able to buy a similar pair for less than eighty pounds.

Some time later Mr. Turner bought a nine bedroom house in Moberly which had had a tennis court in the front garden, this was removed and a new court was put in the back garden. There were a lot of alterations carried out on the house, these alterations were carried out by the same team of workers who did the work on the shops. There was a plasterer, plumber and some joiners and they all came from Swinton and when possible they used to give me lift to Moberly. When this wasn't possible, I would have to catch a train from Piccadilly which dropped me off at Moberly station and then I would have a walk of about a mile to the house.

The work was carried out in the Summer and I would look forward to the early morning walk through the countryside. At lunch time we used to play cricket on the front lawn, one day I was batting and Mr. Turner arrived and came to a halt just short of the orange box that was used as the wicket. Mr. Turner waited until the ball was bowled then said, "you should have had him out that time", he then got out of the car, opened the boot and said, "would you lads like a beer?" and lifted out a crate of beer.

With the house being in the middle of the country it was not connected to the sewers and consequently had its own septic tank which was near the stables. The tank had a two inch steel pipe which went down into the tank which Mr. Turner was trying to lift out and called over for a lift, we raised the pipe, and to his credit he got hold of the sticky end! When we got the pipe out he remarked, "That pongs a bit". Another day he found a wasp's nest in the stables and decided to remove it, he didn't know if it was in use at the time, he got a long stick and knocked the nest to the floor, fortunately it was not inhabited.

On the day that the family moved in they had arranged a buffet for the evening for their friends, but invited the workers for a drink and a bite before we finished for the day. I really enjoyed working on that job.

The Hollies Convent Grammar School
(From "Our James")

In September 1961 work was completed on a new building for the The Hollies Convent Grammar school in Mersey road West Didsbury. The electrical work in the new building was carried out by S. Barratt & Co the company I worked for although I did not work on the installation, I was given the task of completing the architects list of defects, which is the normal procedure on new buildings.

The buildings consisted of the main grammar school, the prep school and the convent. The convent was originally the main house on the estate of a cotton baron, which had a two story coach house.

The coach house became the gardeners' workshop, storage for gardening equipment and canteen.

The staff consisted of the gardener, the gardener's assistant, the caretaker, the joiner and Bob. Bob lived in the Morning Star hostel for homeless men. Bob had a speech impediment and hardly said a word, but was an interesting character, it appeared that Bob had worked with racing horses and I was given the impression that he had had an accident at some stables. When he did talk he spoke about race horses and race courses of which Chepstow came up quite regular. The nuns had given him the job of sweeping the yards etc and kept him fed.

The headmistress at the school was Sister Victoire a typically strict nun. I spent a lot of time working at the Hollies and had a good relationship with her. Although I was attending to the defects I was also constantly being given extra works to be done, additional sockets in many numerable classrooms, chemistry, and physics labs and the two domestic science labs.

I was travelling everywhere by public transport at the time and will never forget one horrendous journey home. It was a very foggy night and I had my bag of tools on my back, the bag was an old back pack. I boarded the bus outside The Hollies which would take me into Manchester. It was a slow journey because of the fog and the nearer we got to Manchester the slower the bus went. We eventually arrived at the Palace Theatre on Oxford Street and the bus ground to a halt, the traffic was gridlocked. I could not see any sense in staying on the bus so decided to walk to Bridge street where I could catch a bus home. (We were living in Beverley Road which is near Agecroft Road at that time). When I reached Bridge Street the traffic was still not moving so I kept on walking. I walked down to Chapel Street, past the cathedral and along to the Crescent and still no sign of a bus. By this time my bag of tools was beginning to take its toll on my shoulders, but I carried on past Peel Park, along Broad Street and along Bolton Road, still no bus had passed me, and eventually reached Beverley Road. We didn't have a phone then as we could not afford one and there were no mobile phones so I was unable to inform Margaret of the situation. The distance I walked was between five and six miles.

I spent a lot of time working at the Hollies and was involved in all kinds of jobs in the classrooms, in the hall, in the pavilion on the field, in the prep school and in the convent.

Every year the school put on a Gilbert and Sullivan opera, Peter Arnfield one of the music teachers taught the singing, one teacher was the producer and the art teachers painted the scenery and provided the props. The lighting for the set was designed by Fr. O'Connor but the actual work of putting the spot lights in position, fitting the colour filters and connecting everything to the dimmer boards was done by me under Fr. O'Connor's instructions. The singing was done by the pupils from the sixth form and men from the teaching staff from The Hollies and Xaverian College, plus contacts of Sr. Victoire and Fr. O'Connor. It was during this time that Kevin (Garner) joined the cast and brought with him Jeff Pierce. This was to be the start of a long friendship which I will return to later.

One year Fr. O'Connor convinced Sr. Victoire that a new dimmer and control board was needed. A representative from "Strand Lighting" specialists in stage lighting came to the school and proposed a completely new system, which I would have to install.

The new system consisted of a main panel which would be installed on the stage below the main fuse board in place of the existing capstan dimmer board. The lighting would be controlled by a three manual portable control board which could be plugged in to a socket box on the stage, or into a socket box in the corridor at the back of the hall so that the person operating the lights would be able to see the lighting effects. Each socket box consisted of two twenty pin sockets for the control circuits and one three pin socket for the mains supply. Two twenty core and one three core cables had to be installed linking the box at the back of the hall to the box on the stage. In the box at the back of the hall I had forty three cables to be soldered to the appropriate connections. The box on the stage, because it had cables coming in and cables going out had eighty six cables to be soldered. You can imagine the amount of work that had to be done, plus I had all the lights to set for the forthcoming opera. To say that it was a close call is an understatement, but I was carrying steps out of the hall as the audience were arriving for the opening night.

I appeared in eight of the operas of which I have many happy memories.

The wooden block floor in the hall was Sr. Victoire's pride and joy and stiletto highheel shoes were not permitted to be worn. There were many local dignitaries invited to the shows and on one occasion the lady mayoress came and had to remove her shoes before she could enter the hall.

A retired deputy head teacher from the school had died and the requiem mass was to be held in the school hall with the senior pupils attending, the requiem Mass was to be said by Bishop Burke. I was working in the school that morning and was called into Sr. Victoire's office who asked me if I would serve the Mass. I was kitted out in a cassock and surplice and that it. I can't remember what I wrote on my time sheet but it was certainly not serving a requiem, for which I got paid for.

Sometimes at the end of the school day Sr. Victoire would appear to relax and would come and engage in conversation. On one occasion she said to me, "If there is going to be any trouble in a school it would inevitably start in the toilets, which is why I inspect the toilets at the end of the day when the pupils have gone home." On one occasion she found somebody had written on the cubicle wall the words "Bay City Rollers." Not being very impressed with this she instructed the art teacher to trace the writing that was on the wall. Next day every class in the school had to write on paper a short composition which was read out by the class teacher. The composition included the words Bay, City and Rollers, but not in that order. Each teacher had been given a copy of the words traced by the art teacher and had to check if any of the pupils in the class had similar writing. Needless to say, the culprit was found and duly punished.

Every year the children in the prep school would play a football match on the field, it would be listed as England v Ireland. Sr. Victoire was a friend of Matt Busby whose grandchildren attended the prep school and each year he would come to the match and present a trophy to the winning team. One year I was there on match day when Matt Busby arrived and he had brought with him a young George Best with his long hair. Sr. Victoire was not too impressed and suggested to George that he should get his hair cut.

Each summer the school would hold a Summer fair, I would be involved with setting up speakers on the flat roofs of the two storey buildings and setting up the equipment for the music. There was also a stall with a large roulette wheel on it which I would have to get an extension lead to.

The annual school speech day was held at "The Free Trade Hall" which has since been converted into The Raddison Hotel. Inevitably I would be asked to help in taking equipment etc to the hall and always received an invitation to the speech night, lots of local political figures including the bishop were in attendance. Sr. Victoire would give an account of the school year and would thank by name all members of the maintenance staff of which I was included.

Christmas was as you can expect another special occasion with all kinds of things doing on, ending with the staff Christmas party to which I was invited and was sent home with a big Christmas cake.

Shay Lane
(From "Our James")

I once had a job in Hale in Cheshire, a new house was being built for a police surgeon on Shay Lane. It was a large house with four or five bedrooms on land facing the Ringway golf course. To get to the site I had to catch a bus into Manchester, then a bus to Altrincham and then a bus to Hale and then a walk across the golf course of about half a mile. This wasn't too bad in the summer, getting up at six o'clock in the morning to get on the site for eight o'clock. The facilities on site were very basic, each trade had his own shed and the builders being the main contractor had a big shed with a wood burning stove with the chimney through the roof. There was a calor gas heater for boiling the kettle for a brew. The toilet consisted of a hole in the ground and a plank of wood to sit on, the smell at any time was revolting and one only visited as a last resort. As winter approached the shell of the house had been built complete with roof the windows and doors had not yet been built. I remember one morning the grass on the golf course was white as snow and by the time I arrived on site I was freezing. I went to put the kettle on but to no avail as the gas in the gas bottle had frozen. Working in the building was a nightmare as the cold wind was blowing through the open windows and doors.

I found that when working in conditions like that, you get home at night and you can feel every little draught, The work progressed and reached the stage when the light fittings could be installed. There was a large open hall with a straight staircase leading to a landing. I had installed a number of light points in line with the staircase, the architect wanted a long flex on each light point. The light at the top of the stairs was about two meters long and each subsequent flex was longer than the previous. Because the flex had come off a drum the flexes would not hang down straight. To rectify this the architect instructed me to tie half a brick to each flex and leave them like that for a few days, after which the weight of the brick had straightened the flex.

Mode Wheel Abattoir
(From "Our James")

While still an apprentice I recall being sent with an electrician to do some work at Mode Wheel abattoir on Salford docks, as it was then. We were working in the area of the slaughter house and could not avoid watching the cattle being killed. The slaughter man would put a bolt gun to the cows head and fire it, the cow would drop to the ground and within five minutes would have its hide removed, its head removed and hung on a hook on the wall, with its tongue hanging out. The cow's innards were removed and the cow cut in two from top to bottom and hung onto hooks on a conveyor track. The whole operation was done so quickly that as the sides of beef went past on the conveyor the nerves of the cow were still twitching. At lunch time we would sit in a corner on our tool boxes and eat our sandwiches, it must have been a Monday because I had meat on mine left over from Sunday dinner.

Pigs were also slaughtered, but they were electrocuted before having their throats slit and were then draped over a large tub to collect the pigs' blood which was used in making black puddings. Sheep like pigs were electrocuted.

I also worked at an abattoir in Leigh and one day one of the sheep escaped, went running down the road and ended up in the nearby canal where it was fished out.

The Rag Trade
(From "Our James")

When I first started work there were still a lot of machine shops in the area where there would be rows of women sat at sewing machines churning out all kinds of clothes. This machinist type of work was referred to as the rag trade.

It was fascinating to watch. There would be an electric motor at one end of a row of sewing machines with a spindle running from one end to the other, each sewing machine was connected to the spindle with a three inch (75mm) wide leather belt. Occasionally there would be a problem with the motor and we would be called out to fix it. The company usually kept a spare motor so it would be a case of remove the faulty motor and replace it with the spare. This work had to be done as quickly as possible as the full line of machinists were idle and losing money as they were all on piece work. i.e. pay was related to the amount of garments produced.

At the time I was working in these premises there was a comedy show on television called "The Rag Trade". I could see most of the characters that were in the show, in the machine shop. Peter Jones (Mr. Fenner The factory boss), Reg. Varney (Foreman) Miriam Carlin (union steward) who at any opportunity would have everybody on strike with what became her clarion call of "everybody out". Other people in the cast were, Sheila Hancock, Barbara Windsor, Gillian Taylforth and Anna Karen.

Littleton Road Flats
(From "Our James")

Barratt's used to do a lot of work with a firm of electrical and mechanical consultants S.I. Sealy, who had won a contract to carry out a survey on corporation houses and flats in Salford. Norman Wood the Electrical consultant had come to an agreement with Barratt's for me to help out with the survey.

I would go with a mechanical engineer and do a survey of each property, he would survey the existing mechanical installation and I would survey the electrical. I would detail number of sockets in each room, cooker points, showers, type of light fittings and standard of decoration in each property.

Each pair of engineers would be given a list of properties to survey, if access could not be made to the property a note would be made and two days later another team would follow up.

One day I was with a big Irishman following up flats where access had not been made. Paddy knocked on one door and immediately let out a groan. He said "this flat has already had a survey carried out" it appeared that the previous team had purposely not signed it off. The door opened and a figure appeared out of the dark corridor of an old woman. She was dirty, had long black straggly hair, only one tooth in the middle of her mouth and only had one eye in her head, where the other eye should have been there was just a hole. The one redeeming feature were the rings on her fingers with stones the size of small rocks.

Her first words were "have you any cigs" followed by "have you any gin". Paddy managed to calm her down and we escaped. He told me that she had been a lady of ill repute who earned her living on the streets.

Some time after the survey had been completed I met one of the mechanical team and we were discussing different things that had happened. I mentioned the lady in the flats and he related the following story.

The lady had died and a joiner was sent to the empty flat to do a mock-up of what the refurbished flat would look like. He let himself into the flat, to see a figure go into the bathroom, he called out but got no reply so he went next door to ask the tenant who was in the flat as he had been informed that the flat was empty. The tenant confirmed that the flat was empty as the lady had died and asked him to describe who he had seen. He replied saying she was dirty, had a hole in her face where her eye should have been and only one tooth in her head!!!!

TALES OF FORTY-SEVEN

Bruntwood Estates
(From "Our James")

Bruntwood Estates was a difficult company to deal with, whatever estimate you presented they would always want it reduced, and always haggled if any additional work was required. I once gave them an estimate for tracing some circuits in a multi occupied building which could only be carried out on a Saturday. The work did not take as long as I estimated and the Bruntwood surveyor was aware of this and wanted a reduction in the estimate. I asked him, if it had taken longer would he have paid more money. "Certainly not" was his reply. I said "you can't have the cake and eat it so the answer is no". That is the kind of thing they did.

Bruntwood had moved offices to a building they had bought called "Abney Hall" which is in its own grounds Cheadle.

It used to be the home of S & J Watts family who were cotton merchants in Manchester. Uncle Wilf used to work for them at one time. He told me that they were not nice to work for. He told me, that the boss would walk round and if he didn't like the look of somebody he would tell them to collect their cards.

It was a magnificent building with chandeliers on winches that you could wind down for maintenance and changing lamps. The roof space was huge and could easily have been converted to more rooms. There were as many rooms in the cellar as there were on the ground floor.

Once during the winter two new pumps had been installed for the heating and I had been given an electrician to wire them up. I was assured that he knew what he was doing. I received a call telling me that the pumps were not working and had to go to Abney Hall to find out why. There were two what we call three phase pumps, one for each pump, there was a starter unit for each pump. When I removed the covers of the starters I found that the wiring was connected up wrong and that the pumps had burnt out. With parts of the hall sub- let to tenants plus Bruntwood staff, I realised that it was a major problem and that there would be an enquiry and whoever was responsible would have to pay. I disconnected the wiring in each starter and re-connected them as they should have been. Bruntwood sent an electrical consultant to inspect the pumps and the wiring and then I was instructed to attend a meeting with Mike Ogglesby (Sir Michael), the architect and the electrical consultant to try to establish what had gone wrong. I remember that at one stage Mike Ogglesby told me to stop waffling, but they never did find out what really was the cause.

Adsega
(From "Our James")

In the early 1960s a chain of small supermarket shops was set up in the northwest, they were established in existing premises in shopping areas like Northenden, Patricroft and Salford. The one in Salford which was the first supermarket to be opened was in the old Bijou cinema on Broughton road opposite the steps which led to Whit Lane.(When the Bijou was a cinema they used to show silent films, the films were accompanied by a pianist playing music to match the action on the screen. My Mams sister, Aunty Margaret used to play the piano at the Bijou and also alternated playing at the Ambasador cinema on Langworthy road with Violet Carson, who ended up playing Enna Sharples in Coronation street.) I worked on the Adsega in Northenden and was sent on my own to the one in Patricroft. I remember the owner came to the site in Northenden. The company was bought along with a number of other supermarket shops by Tesco.

Bayer Dyestuffs
(From "Our James")

Bayer's was a member of the German Bayer group of companies which is connected to the Bayer Levercusen football club.

The company was based on Washway Road in Sale and had huge vats where compounds were coloured with various coloured dyes. It was almost impossible to work there and not get covered in some of the dye. They had a three story flameproof tower built where they stored highly inflamable chemicals. Everything in the building had to be fireproof, light fittings, switches, sockets and even the telephone.

The manager was a decent man and would always give me a bottle of wine at Christmas if I was working there. Sometimes I would have to go to his house in Altrincham to carry out electrical works. I was working there one day when I had to remove items from under the stairs to carry out the work. Amongst them was a wooden farmyard which had a farmhouse and a number of buildings for the animals and in the middle was a painted duck pond. Also under the stairs was a Noah's Ark. Both items were quality toys and when I had finished the lady of the house asked if I could find use for them. We kept the farm for some time and eventually gave it to St. Luke's school. As I am writing this the ark is in "The room" where Grace still plays with it.

REMINISCENSES

All Saints Primary School Mosses Gate
(From "Our James")

In May 1963 I was given the job of carrying out the installation to a new primary school in Farnworth, at the time we were living in Beverley Road which suited me down to the ground. Travelling time and expenses were measured from the office which at the time was in Altrincham street near London road station, so I was claiming more than I was paying out which was a change.

One of the workers I had on site was Frank Barratt, the boss's son who was a bit of pain even then.

The garden which we had inherited at Beverley Road was in a bit of a state, I had to dig all the weeds out to start with I then needed to flatten the soil before I could put some turf down. I discussed this with Frank and he helped me to make a garden roller out of a large oil can and filled with cement, which when it was finished he took it to our house in his car, which at the time was a Morris Minor.

I can still see the school today as I drive on the motorway to Bolton.

Tootal Broadhurst Lee
(From "Our James")

In 1964 Mr. Barratt bought out a well established electrical contractor called Broughton & Irlam who were based in Salford, which included contracts which were still in progress. One of the contracts was at Tootal Broadhurst Lee on Oxford street in Manchester. It was and still is a five story red brick building. The job was to install a new four hundred line internal telephone system in the building, which was being supervised by an electrician who worked for Broughton and Irlam. It was very interesting from my point of view as I had not been involved with any telephone installations.

Memories of 47
(From "Our Angela")

Dear Anthony,

You and James have inspired me to pour forth some memories of 47. Here they are so far!

Earliest memory – Lying on the settee with Pete and a white bundle – baby Joe. We all had measles.

Balancing on planks in the kitchen to get from the lobby door to the back door. Mam had complained that the little ones couldn't walk properly because the floor was uneven so my Dad had taken up the flags and concreted the newly levelled floor.

Standing in the front room next to the toy red desk with metal frame and matching stool. I was crying because we had been told we couldn't use it as a playroom anymore because it was going to be decorated.

The whole family going to Eccles on the bus to have the family photograph taken. Pete and I had to sit on a pink box. It was very bumpy and most uncomfortable. Joe was crying so the lady gave him a toy duck to play with. Look very carefully at the photo and you will see it in his hand. In 1978 when we had the family photo taken at the Old Boy's, I took a plastic duck for Joe and he sat it on his knee! A week after we had the original photo taken I went to Eccles with my Mam to collect the prints. There was a copy of our photo outside the shop in a glass case.

Going upstairs to bed when I was about 3 years old. I passed a man on the stairs. I asked Pauline, "Who's that?" "It's Gerard. He's one of the big ones," she replied. I think he was newly returned from the navy and I didn't know him.

Watching Mary packing a suitcase in the bedroom. I remember her taking a green musical box off the mantlepiece and putting it in her case. I was upset because I really liked that musical box and didn't understand why it had to go in the case. Then I saw the case in the back kitchen on Dad's chair. Mary got her coat down off the hook on the kitchen door. I asked, "Where are you going Mary?" She said, "Oh, I'll be back soon." About 5 years ago, on a visit here, Mary said, "I have something for you." It was the green musical box, exactly as I remembered it, and it is now one of my most treasured possessions.

Going to Liverpool with Mr. Marshall to wave Mary off. She stood on deck and waved to us.

Having the afternoon off school to go to Liverpool to wave Anthony off to Canada.

Being sent next door to welcome Mr. Marshall home. Apparently he had been in the army! (Prison)

Mrs. Sharp giving us empty Kellogs boxes so that we could cut the free masks out.

Sundays. The hustle and bustle to get the lads out in time for 11.00 Mass. Roast beef for dinner with rice pudding made in a big pyrex dish. The little ones had their pudding on a saucer. Running with James to Sunday School at St Philip's. Rushing to get tea ready so that the lads could get to church in time for Compline, Sermon and Benediction. We always had salad for tea and tinned fruit with carnation cream. Also cakes that Mam had baked. Even the bread tasted special on Sundays. It was years later that I discovered that this was because on Sunday we had butter on the bread instead of margarine! John used to take some of the cakes in an empty Kellogs box to church for the priests.

Christmas. We couldn't wait to close the curtains on Christmas Eve because then we knew it was nearly Christmas. I hated the smell of 6lb of onions boiling in a pan to make the stuffing. I loved the smell of the cooked stuffing when we came back from midnight Mass and had stuffing butties.

Our first real Christmas tree. When Tom and Anthony came home with it I asked my Dad where he had got it from. Dad said you had to know where to stand and they fell from the sky. You just had to catch one. I had a wonderful image in my head. I think the tree had actually come from Babyfair on Broad Street.

Presents I remember. Pete and John got boxing gloves and a punch ball fixed to a plank. My pink carry cot. Doll's house furniture to go in the doll's house that came from Brentwood, wheeled home by Anthony on the old trolley. We always got an apple, a satsuma, some nuts, a selection box, a book and a shiny sixpence. I believe the latter was from Mrs Sharp. One year I got a brilliant pink easel and blackboard. I think James had made it at woodwork and it had been on the shelter roof all night so that the paint would dry. Other presents – a cowboy/girl suit for me and Joe, Tap-tap for Pete, a ranch and an electric train for Joe.

The first one to wake up would then wake the rest of us. We would creep downstairs to the front room, look at our presents then go outside to look back through the window to see Baby Jesus in the crib.

John and Angela

Bonfire night. Collecting wood weeks before bonfire night. Sending Joe to ask the big ones, "Penny for the guy." The money they gave him paid for our fireworks. Making a guy with Dad's old overalls. Mam making the best treacle toffee and toffee apples. Waiting impatiently for Dad to come home from work so he could light the fire.

When Joe was about 5 years old the road outside the kitchen window had to be dug up. It was a big job and lasted some time. Joe spent most of his time outside watching the workmen. Eventually they let him join them in their canvas shelter for a brew and at the end of the week they gave him a pay packet with money in it.

One bad winter it was so cold that the toilet bowl broke. Fortunately Mrs Marshall let us use theirs until we got a new one. We had to go out the back door, along the entry then up the steps into Marshall's back yard. When we got the new toilet Dad put an oil heater in there. It was the warmest room in the house. It was so cold sometimes that in the bedroom and bathroom the net curtains froze onto the windows with ice on the inside.

Mam used to do the washing in the cellar with a copper boiler and mangle. It used to take her all day. When Joe was very young he fell down the cellar steps while Mam was washing and hurt his head. After that we got an electric machine in the kitchen. One time when a repair man came to fix it Mam fell over his tool box and broke her arm. On wash day we used to have to throw the bed sheets down stairs to be washed. They were in a big pile at the bottom of the stairs. We used to jump off the stairs and land on the washing. I remember the great sense of achievement when I finally plucked up the courage to jump off the tenth stair.

Dad used to leave for work at about 6.30am. We hated the weather forecasts he used to shout up the stairs in the winter. "There's six inches of snow out there." "It's thick with fog. You can't see to walk. There'll be no buses." "It's pouring down." Who wanted to get up out of bed after that?

Dad came home at about 6.00pm. We had to listen out for his bell as he rode past the kitchen window then one of us had to rush to open the front door just in time for him to bring his bike in. He would sit on his chair and put his feet up while we undid the laces on his boots. Then he gave us empty sweet wrappers. We had to use the back of a tea spoon to flatten out the silver paper from them then put them in the small oven space in the fire range. I'm not sure why we collected silver paper. I think maybe it was for the blind?

One evening, sitting on the bottom stair with Pete and staring excitedly at the closed front door. Tom was due home from the Air Force. At last there was a knock on the door and we ran to open it. There stood Tom in his uniform with his kit bag in his hand. Pete and I practically dragged him into the front room saying, "Play that thing on the piano where your hands go up and down all the time." Sparkling Cascades. Tom duly obliged, still wearing his cap. We were absolutely delighted. He brought back a beautiful black lacquered musical box and a parasol for Mam, a red satin pyjama set for Margaret and a miniature tea set for me. I still have it. It is in perfect condition.

One year Dad bought a do-it-yourself chimney cleaning kit. There was a brush on a stick then a series of metre long sticks that screwed into each other as the brush was pushed up the chimney. We came home from school one day to see the brush sticking out of the top of the middle room chimney. When Dad had tried to pull it down one of the sticks had come unscrewed and fallen off. He couldn't reach up the chimney to get hold of the next one. Joe, who was the smallest, was helped/pushed up the chimney in the middle room to reach the next stick and pull it down. Dad didn't try cleaning chimneys again.

One year it was decided that the front of the house should be painted red. And so it happened and it looked good. But then somebody had the brilliant idea that we needed white lines painted in between every brick! It was the job of the young ones to do this. It took forever. I remember spending many hours with Pete in the summer holidays painting these white lines. We had a jam jar of white paint and a small paintbrush. I don't remember if it was ever completely finished.

There was certainly a space up near the gutters that was unfinished for quite a while.

One hot summer day Anthony decided to do some sunbathing. He climbed out onto the bay roof outside the boy's bedroom. He was wearing a pair of mini bathing trunks. (*It was actually a bikini, which I had bought in Nice, and at the time was very proud of it!..Anthony*)He lay down on a towel to enjoy the sun. Suddenly we heard the noise of a brass brand getting closer and closer. I think it was St. Barnabus' procession and I'm not sure if Uncle Frank wasn't playing in the band. Anthony tried to sneak back through the window but somebody, I can't remember who, was quicker than him and locked the window. He had to stay out there while the procession slowly made its way past the house with many people gazing up at the wonderful sight on the bay roof.

REMINISCENSES

Every Wednesday Mam used to go to the Co-op (pronounced Cworp] to get the rations. We had to meet her there when we came out of school at dinner time. She had the old trolley with a big cardboard box on it. It was filled with food. We had to help to carry the other shopping bags home. The shopping included sugar in blue bags, loose leaf tea, Gold Seal margarine and loose biscuits in paper bags. I'm sure other shoppers dreaded standing behind Mam in the queue because her list was so long. She wrote it all down in a little notebook.

   39614, 4169 * These were our Co-op numbers
   PEN 4867 This was our telephone number

Sometimes when we answered the phone we would hear the operator say, "You have a call from Canada."

At that time calls had to be booked in advance and lasted for just 3 minutes then the operator would cut the line. If you answered one of these calls you had to stand there holding the phone and yelling at the top of your voice, "Mam. It's Canada. Hurry up." There was just about enough time for us all to say hello to Mary then we were cut off.

At meal times we all sat around the table together then Mam would start serving the food in order of importance – big ones first then the little ones who had to sit on the form. One day I was feeling especially thirsty and couldn't wait for our turn. I had the impertinence to start to pour myself a cup of tea. Anthony, who was sitting at the head of the table, yelled, "What the blazes do you think you're doing?" He then snatched my cup up off the table. What he didn't realise was that I had already put the milk in the cup. It went all over

Anthony. I didn't know whether to laugh or cry. There were stifled laughs from around the table. Mam said to Anthony, "Serves yourself right." Phew! Thanks Mam.

One evening Mam and Dad went out. A rare occurrence. They came home in a taxi. Dad's best suit was covered in flour. They had been to the Free Trade Hall with the Co-op where they were recording a popular radio show called 1/- a Second. Before the show they asked the audience if anybody had 20 children. Nobody. They went down the numbers until they got to 12. The other people in Dad's group shouted, "Up here." Mam and Dad were then invited to take part in the show. I'm not sure how it worked but they had to answer questions, it was timed and a bag of shillings was involved. If they got a question wrong they had to do a forfeit. They won a blanket, a bedside table, a barometer and a bag of shillings. The question they got wrong was which is the smallest county in England? Rutland. They had to do a forfeit. An igloo was brought onto the stage. Dad had to crawl inside and Mam had to pour bags of flour down the chimney. When they came home we all sat round the radio in absolute silence and listened to the show. I remember Margaret having to brush Dad's suit down. The flour was everywhere – in his pockets, under the collar, in his turn ups and in his hair. In the end the suit had to go to the cleaners.

Dad won the pools. It was a charity pools called "The Spastics". He won £1088 10 shillings and 8 pence. Mam and Dad took Joe to Canada by boat because Dad refused to go by plane. The trip was booked through Uncle James who was a shipping clerk and they went on a Manchester Liners ship from Salford docks. These were cargo ships but took up to a dozen passengers on board. Mam, Dad and Joe went off to the docks with their suitcases. Those of us who were left at home ie James, Pauline, John, Peter and me went down to the docks on the bus – No 72? We were allowed in the cabins then said our farewells. We went home for dinner then got a bus to Barton Swing Bridge. We waited on the tow path then saw the huge ship making its way down the canal. It was so big it practically filled the canal. We could almost reach out and touch it. As it got closer we could see Mam, Dad, Joe and other passengers standing at the front of the ship. We were hanging over the fence waving and shouting, "Come back. We haven't had our dinner." I don't know what the Captain and other passengers made of this sight!

August 1971. One morning a man arrived with a clip board. He went in every room in the house, looking around and making notes. It was one of the worst feelings ever. This was it. It was real. It was really happening. The Compulsory Purchase Order.

September 1974. Mam and Dad moved out of 47 to go to Overdale. Gerard drove them in his car. He said Dad sat there in tears with the clock on his knee all the way to their new house.

Harry Marshall
(From Anthony)

In previous episodes mention has been made of our next-door neighbour, so now maybe it's time to talk about:

We first became aware of Harry when the Malteser moved out of the property opposite us, and shortly thereafter Harry Marshall moved in to the premises. At that time he lived in New Chapel Street, which was not the most salubrious street in the area. Later, in 1954 he bought the house next door to us #49.

One of the many memorable things about him was his use of nick-names. One of the (not so successful) dealers who used to come there, wore glasses like the bottom of coke bottles. I can't tell you his name because I don't think anyone knew it, because Marshall always called him Twink. One time Marshall had to go to his house, and when they got there realised they didn't know his name, didn't think they could ask for Twink if his missus came to the door, suddenly remembered his first name, was Ernie & were prepared to use that if he didn't answer the door.....he did! They were saved! Anyway, one day Ernie Twink arrives at Marshall's to ask his opinion on a vehicle that Twink had "fixed?" up. HM points to the dash where the speedometer should be and says: What the 'ells that? Twink says oh its an altimeter (out of a plane – shows how high you are!), and then adds the comment that:

"Wot the 'eck, most of them bloody things don't work, no-one will notice." After inspecting the vehicle, HM suggested that the best thing Twink could do was to drive around the Crescent, and the first time he sees a Corporation Bus over the double lines, smash into it, cause they are well insured!

Harry (& Bert his assistant) worked on the week-end, all day Saturday, and about 10.00 – 4pm on Sunday. There were three females who objected to "working on the Sabbath". One was an elderly lady in a wheelchair, and presumably the others were her (unhappy looking) daughters who at that time looked old to me, although they were probably only in their fifties. Any way these three decided to come and sing hymns outside Harry's garage, for which they were nicknamed Faith, Hope and Charity. After their initial appearance it quickly got to the point that when they arrived, Harry would bellow: "Bert! Faith Hope and Charity are here" which was the signal for Bert to get an electric sander and start sanding the wing of a car (a most horrible racket) and they soon disappeared!

In his yard, Harry always had an Alsation dog, it was a pet and was guard dog only in the sense that it would bark and let him know someone was around. It certainly wasn't a vicious dog. One of the dealers who used to come was named Len Goodier, and he just happened to have a big hooter(nose). He often used to tease the dog, and just as often was told not to, but he carried on until...........one day Ranger sunk his teeth right into that big hooter.

Of course Len Goodier has blood coming out of his nose, is very unhappy and moaning and groaning. Harry's sympathy extended to: "What's wrong with you, the dogs teeth weren't in there for long!........ and in any case I warned you!"

Re nick-names, there was a lady lived nearby who unfortunately had one thin leg and one fat one. In addition she was a bit blowsy, and while she was unaware of the nickname she was referred to as "Scrumptious". Her children walked funnily and were known as Penguin and little penguin.

There was also a blonde babe who used to visit, and we children were told it was his "cousin" (which it definitely was not!) Some of the other nicknames: Screaming Mouth Almighty, – a lady who talked extremely loudly, and also used lots of malapropisms (e.g. Pakispaniards for Pakistanis), Billypot – a man who always wore a Bowler hat (in fact one day he came to our house to talk to my Dad, Pete answered the door, and promptly shouted, Dad, Mr Billypot wants to talk to you) Many years later we found out his name was Mr Brumby. There was also a pedlar- a lady – who was a very long way from the front when good looks were given out. She was kind of bent over, black straggly hair, weird glasses (and I think that's what she sold – my Dad nick-named her Rosie tea leaves. I guess you had to be there to appreciate it.

In our eyes he was a very good man and did lots of good for us children. He bought a single decker bus and converted it into a caravan, towed it to Rhyl in North Wales, and his wife and family used to spend the summer holidays there. However, he often used to take some of us there for a week-end.

One time he bought a double-decker bus and converted it into a caravan, Decided to take it to Rhyl (where he sold it) and because of low bridges had to go a different route.

Somewhere near Chester I had to get out of the truck, go and stand under a bridge, and slowly motion to him to go ahead whilst watching to see if there was enough clearance. While I am doing this, some old geezer, sitting on a bench, says, "It's alright it'll fit". I asked him how he knew, and the response was "Cause this is a bus route!!!" grr.

Another time, coming home from Rhyll, me, Tom and Neville are in the back of this five-ton lorry. There's a little old Austin seven doing his damndest to pass us, and we, of course are waving to the driver. He managed to pass us and promptly stopped to give Harry a speeding ticket! We got "what for" because we were supposed to be keeping an eye out for the cops!!

One time at Rhyll I went out shooting rabbits with young Harry while his Dad was at a farm…we didn't get any rabbits, but his Dad brought back bacon and eggs (which were rationed at the time). Guess it was a black market trip!

There was another chap that used to come to Harry Marshall's. Unlike most of Marshall's visitors he was well dressed. He was Jewish and his name was Harry Tobias although we kids knew him as Toby (or Mr Toby). One of the reasons he appealed to me was because he paid well to have his car cleaned, but he used to stand at our front watching the little ones play and was very impressed at how well they got along. One day he asked my Mam (I wasn't there – I was on the croft playing football) if he could take the children for a ride, she said yes but after a couple of hours began to wonder where they were, and I suspect she was a little bit worried. When they did get home, she found out he had taken them to Clevelys (about 50 miles away) and paid for rides on the fair ground!)

Reverting back to Harry's caravan, there was a time when Bert (and by the way Bert had a very decided squint in one eye, and could stand at the corner and look up both sides of the street at one time – well not really, but that's what we always thought) was hammering away at some plywood, making a heck of a noise. My Mam called across the road and said "What are you making Bert" to which he replied "a touse". This, of course, puzzled my Mam and she said " a touse. what's a touse?" The response – A shithouse.

Unwittingly I provided a lot of laughter for Marshall. No matter how late anyone came home at night, they probably weren't heard, except for me! Because whenever I got home late next door's dog started to bark, and Ellen Marshall told my Mam that Harry used to lie there in bed laughing like crazy and saying Anto's in trouble again!

One day I was in the kitchen at "47" with my Mam and others, when Harry Marshall walked down the lobby, came in the kitchen and told my Mam he'd come to borrow Ten Pounds! Well he knew darn well that there would be no Ten Quid in our house, however he just grinned, took a pile of bank-notes out of his inside pocket and extracted 10 quid. It seems he told someone that was all the money he had and had to borrow the money to do the deal!

When he went to the sales of ex-army vehicles I often went with him and one day we went to Boston Spa on the grounds of an estate (Harewood Hall) that had been commandeered during the war. This was where I first saw a fox hunt or at least the group who were doing it. I looked up at this man (red jacket etc) on a great big horse and said "Ow many dogs you got mister?" To which he replied "HOUNDS boy HOUNDS!" At these sales everything was for cash and I have never seen so much money in my life. I was sent to pay a bill for Harry Marshall and the Five Hundred pounds never left my clutching hand until it was passed to the cashier. The man in front of me was paying a big bill, he was wearing a duffle coat and I remember him digging into various pockets...there's 500, there's another 700, there's another whatever. Behind the counter the money was stashed on the floor and it was stacked 4 feet high! There must have been millions! One day someone (I think it was our Tom) said "ay look over there". The were two men at Marshall's buying a car, looked familiar, turned out to be Spider & Billy Austin, clowns from Belle Vue circus.

This next item doesn't really concern HarryMarshall, but rather his wife Ellen. One night I brought a couple of friends home about 11 o clock on a Saturday night. M & D were in bed, and we decided to have some chips and persuaded our Margaret to make them. We were in the front room. playing records, when we heard this blood-curdling scream; I dashed into the kitchen and there's Margaret with a pan of blazing fat. I took it outside and dumped it, fat and all, into the dustbin. So there we were with a bowl of raw chips and no chip pan. In those days when you put your chip pan away you left the fat in it, so I simply went next door and asked Ellen Marshall if we could borrow her chip pan (this is sometime after 11:00pm at night) – so we did get our chips.

Another time Harry Marshall had a lot of batteries in his garage, and was saying to me that he was concerned because if anyone broke in the easiest thing to steal was the batteries, and wondered if he could store them in our cellar. This was before Harry bought the house next door to us, anyway I asked my Dad, who not only agreed, but put up a shelf in our cellar, especially for the batteries, and they were all passed down through the coal hole (the same one my Mam got stuck in another time) to be stored there safely, away from any thieves. Imagine my Dad's horror when many years later Harry Marshall was sent to prison for receiving stolen property, to wit: car engines and batteries!!

One time Harry had a whole slew of tyre chains (for snowy weather) which had come with the ex-army vehicles he had bought at sales, and he said I could have them and sell them to Cox & Danks. There were a lot of them and they were heavy, so I offered our Tom a shilling if he would help me. I had no idea what they were worth so I thought I was taking a bit of a gamble. Well we got the trolley and struggled our way uphill to Cox & Danks the scrap merchants. Well, it wasn't quite as easy as we had envisaged. First they asked where we got them from, then where does he live, and does he have a telephone number, then the guy dis-appeared for a while. It was probably years later that we figured out that he thought they were stolen, and went to check up on us. When he did return he paid me about 31 shillings. So we got home and I gave Tom his shilling. Obviously, my Mam didn't think very much of this and told me that wasn't very fair, and I responded that on Sunday at Mass they had told the parable of the vineyard when everybody got paid the same amount, regardless of what they did.........Yes, you are right in what you are thinking. That didn't wash with my Mam, but I honestly don't remember how much we each got (I probably got a bit more than Tom) because, of course most of it finished up with my Mam. Well, I think that finishes the saga of Harry Marshall, and so I should return to "47."

Locked Out!

Our Pete told the story of M & D being locked out, but that wasn't the only lock-out story, there are more. Before I get to the actual tales, you must realise that although there was a lock on the front door, there was also a sliding bolt. Our house was safer than the Bank of England, and I remember harry Marshall laughing about this, when he said something like: Your house is as impregnable as Fort Knox, and I really don't understand why; there's clearly no money to be snitched, and I couldn't imagine anyone trying to break into a house that has your Dad and eight lads in it...........they'd be crackers!!

One night around Christmas/New Year Tom and I were going out to parties after going skating. I realised I didn't have my front door key and usually I got home after Tom(we were going to different parties) so I suggested that when he got home, after he opened the door to leave his key on the ledge above the door. Well I got home, felt for the key and it wasn't there. I figured there were 7 boys in the front bedroom so surely I could wake one of them up.(Dreamer!) Stones on the window didn't work and finally I had to hammer on the door....Who eventually opens the door but my Dad. "What time do you call this?" he said, "er I don't know." He grabs my watch and said I should have spent the balance of the night where I'd been until now(it was probably around 4.00am). Anyway I was in trouble. I went into the bedroom to give Tom a piece of my mind....and he wasn't home yet...the dirty stopout. I could have waited another hour and not got in trouble.

Another time, on the way home I realised I didn't have my key. So I stopped at the phone box at the roundabout by Cromwell/Littleton Road. You have to realise that in those days you put your tuppence in the box, dialled your number, and when the person answered you had 2 choices. If you had the wrong number you could press Button B and get your money back, or if the right number press Button A and make the connection. Now I knew that my Dad would never get out of bed to answer the phone, also as it was below the boy's bedroom the chances are that a boy would hear it and answer. It happened that this time it was Tom who answered. As soon as he answered I pressed Button B, got my money back, left the phone hanging, Meanwhile I ran like the clappers in time to see Tom through the front room window still saying "Press button A" until I tapped on the window to say its only me, let me in.

Another time I did have my key, got home, put key in lock, turned and the #**$& door wouldn't open. Because someone had bolted it! Well, once again I had to hammer on the door, and once again it was my Dad who let me in! After receiving a good telling off, I went into our bedroom, lifted Tom's head from the pillow by grabbing his hair, and let it fall. After about three of these Tom woke up, er yeah what? I said "were you the last one in?"..Tom; "Yes." "Did you bolt the door?" Tom": Yes" Me: "You clown, I was still out!"

The format of this tale changes somewhat now, and I will try to cover the areas which I have missed.

During our early days in Walsall St, I'm guessing I'd be about 4 or 5, and young enough to do whatever I am told to do by my elders (who would have been 6 & 8!), Mary decided to have a tea party (Using dolls teapot & cups). It was all set up on an inverted orange box, in front of the fireplace in our bedroom. Unusually there was a fire in the grate (big mistake), and of course there had to be a lace tablecloth (probably an old net curtain). This was only possible because my Mam had gone down to Number 1 or to the co-op. Somehow the tablecloth caught fire! It was soon extinguished, but someone had to race down to number one to tell my Mam. In all our later discussions that is one thing I forgot to ask my Mam about, but presume she was somewhat shocked.

Another Mary story. Again she would have been very young, 6,7, or 8. Saturday morning, M & D are having a lie-in, and Mary decides to give them a big treat, and goes downstairs and makes a cup of coffee. Years later we heard the sequel. My Dad tastes the coffee (after Mary has left) and says "ugh it's awful" Mam says : oh go on with you get it down you, she has tried very hard to do something special for you. Dad duly sups the coffee (probably making strange faces). When they get downstairs, Mam asks Mary "what did you make that coffee with?" Mary told her, she made it with the bottle Mam usually used (thinking Camp Coffee which comes in a bottle), and when Mam asked Mary to show her the bottle, she did......................It was a bottle of Gravy browning!!!!

When Mary was in Standard one at St Sebastian's she started a tradition. Her teacher at the time (a Miss Hart) had commented that the scissors they were using seemed to be blunt; Mary quickly volunteered and told the teacher that her Dad was very clever and he could sharpen all kinds of things. So Mary arrives home one day with thirty pairs of scissors for her Dad to sharpen. Remember Mary was the first of twelve, so my Dad was kept busy for many years!

I was a fairly frequent customer at Salford Royal Hospital. In my first year at school (like playschool here in Canada) when I would be 3 or 4, I dashed wanting to be the first in line, when the infants teacher came out to ring the bell, however I was too quick and she brought the bell down and it landed on my head , splitting it open. They put a plaster on it and someone was sent for my Mam who took me to Salford Royal (which entailed two buses) don't know why ambulances weren't even thought of. Anyway they put two stitches in my head, and when we got back home it was close to quitting time at school, so I had to stand on the croft, with my Mam, so she could show Miss Paton that I was OK. I heard later that the poor teacher thought she had killed me!!

Years passed, and when I was about 12 yrs old, there was some kind of a melee in the school yard, at playtime, and I either tripped or was pushed, and my head landed on the clog of someone who was on the ground (It must have been a fight). Once again, off to Salford Royal (and it certainly wasn't anyone like Florence Nightingale that treated me!) The Sister in charge was more like Hatti Jacques in Carry On Nurse. First they put six stitches in the gash, didn't like something about it, took them out and replaced them with two big stitches, and if I even whimpered (and I may have done) I was told to be quiet, and not be so soft (and I'm sure they didn't use any painkiller). Eventually that gash became septic so I was able to have a few days off school!!

Whilst on a medical kick, you should hear about Gerard. He had started work at Platt's or Massey Ferguson in Trafford Park (the industrial site which was the pre-cursor to the Trafford Centre). He went to work on his bike and one day, being in pain came home (on his bike) and by then he was in agony.

I don't remember if my Mam called the doctor or the ambulance, but in short order Gerard had surgery for appendicitis. He had lots of guts did our Gerard.

Considering we are on a medical theme, perhaps this is where I should tell about my Dad's very severe cold! One night after tea my Dad was complaining about having a real bad cold (and he did not handle ill health very well). Any way, he had a brain wave and recalled that he had heard that rum was good for a cold. Bear in mind my Dad was NOT a drinker. Once in a while he might have a half of mild at the club, otherwise he would have either Bristol Cream sherry or Sandeman's port at Christmas (hence a bottle might well last more than a year). There happened to be a bottle of Navy rum (belonged to Gerard) which was VERY strong in the cupboard, so Dad gets a glass, and in one gulp (cause its medicine) swallows about two ounces, neat! Within a very short time he felt like he was dying and asked Mam to call the doctor – which she did. He told the doctor about his absolutely splitting headache, and on the side Mam told him about the rum. The doctor laughed, and told my Mam he was DRUNK!!! (probably for the first time ever!)

Several of the family were involved in processions & May Queen things. Mary was a maid of honour, Gerard, Tom, Neville, and Joe were cushion bearers and there may have been others. The prize appearance in this area though has to go to Angela. Angela was the May Queen, and her cushion bearer was Kevin Garner – she didn't know then that he would eventually be her husband. On Angela's train there was the coat of arms of the Mathers.

The Prior at St Sebastian's for some years was Fr. Fabian Dix who was a great admirer of things medieval, and incorporated some of that in his processions. One time he had a jester (me) in the procession, and another priest Fr. Placid Croney once told my Mam that the funniest thing he ever saw in his life was a Roman slave riding his bike at top speed down Rugely St.......that was my only claim to fame!

Another change of pace! Now we'll talk about the house itself...Number 47. Obviously there has been a great change in many things since we moved into 47, and some readers may not be aware that in those days it was very rare for a working class family to own their own house. I would not be surprised if some working class folk thought that a mortgage was a possession that rich people owned. Anyway my Mam had heard that Mr Gregory was considering selling our house and next door. Now Mr Gregory was a greengrocer on Broughton Rd, so one day, having heard what Mam had said, I went into the shop and spoke to him. I asked how much he wanted, suggested that my Mam & Dad ought to get a break as sitting tenants, and also pointed out that the house had a big crack in the back wall running down from the girls bedroom to the kitchen. went home and told my Mam. I don't really know exactly how it happened, but this much I do know. My Dad discussed it with Mr Woolley JP who was the President of the Pendleton Co-op board of which my Dad was a member. At one meeting, my Dad was asked to leave the room, as they were going to discuss business concerning him. When he was called back in, the President congratulated him, and told him that the Board had agreed to grant him a mortgage! I do recall that my Dad came home happy as could be and then the deal was formalised. This was in 1969. I,m fairly sure that they got the house for either 200 or 250 pounds.

At the time we moved in, the back kitchen floor sloped, and was made of flag stones about 3ft square. My Dad decided to improve this, and (assisted mostly by Tom) took up the flagstones, leveled off the dirt, which was a bit of a problem because a lead pipe (for water) ran diagonally across the floor from the door to the sink. Then he laid some heavy duty paper (with a lining of silver paper) which I think was the stuff used at work for shipping machinery abroad. And after that they mixed concrete and presto! we had a new floor, and that's why, in Pete's story he mentions the step down into the kitchen, it stems from the floor leveling.

Another improvement was making a service hatch between the kitchen and the middle room. That would be easy to do here in Canada because dividing walls are made from 2 x 4s and plaster board, but at 47 the dividing wall was brick,so for someone with no construction experience it was a tricky operation. Yet another major problem was when there was a back-up in the drain in the cellar. Dad spoke to someone at the town hall, they checked, and didn't know what the cause was. They said they would look into it, but if the fault was in our house Dad would have to pay!

Well, they certainly looked into it, and at that time I don't remember seeing much heavy duty machinery (e.g.diggers, bulldozers etc). One day a bunch of workmen arrived and started digging on London Street, they dug down by hand – (navvies) and went down 17 feet where they found the sewer, which was blocked. The sewer was wooden, and was laid in 1875, and had survived a land mine (which destroyed a school about 150 yards away as well as houses only twenty yards away). This was actually our Joe's first job for the city, because my Mam used to brew tea for these workers, especially on a cold day (when she would pour some of my scotch in it!), and our Joe would take it down to them, He also stood around the brazier which the night watchman had to keep him warm. People were paid in cash weekly at that time, so when they got their pay packets these chaps had a collection and put money in an envelope, giving it to Joe, telling him that was his wages! So that's why I say it was his first job working for the Corporation!

Travel

Mention has already been made about my Mam going to Canada for health reasons when she was young, however the more I think about travel, the more I realise what a vast change has happened just in my short life.

During the forties and fifties it was almost unheard of for a person from a working class family to go abroad, that seemed to be reserved for the wealthy. Compare that to the current situation where most people reading this will quite possibly have travelled half way round the world!

In our family I was the first of our lot to go abroad. My friends were going to Squires Gate (a holiday camp similar to Butlins) at Blackpool, and I couldn't afford that, so I decided to go to France and Belgium on my bike. Clearly I hadn't thought it out in great detail, thinking that I could stay in Youth Hostels (even though I hadn't checked to see what towns had youth hostels!) This was in 1951 and of course not very long after the war so many things weren't organised as well as they would be later. At some stage Cyril Barlow asked if he could come with me and I agreed. Rather than including a travel novel in this space, suffice it to say that we went Dover-Ostend – Bruges Brussels -Paris -Calais and home. In the two weeks we were away we slept in 2 youth hostels, a couple of haystacks, camped in the centre of Paris (on a bombed site) were put up in a shed and in someones home and in something like the YMCA.

Mary was the next one to travel and she went to Switzerland (on the train not on a bicycle). Gerard and Olive went to Austria (I think) on their honeymoon, and there was more travel which will be included in the part dealing with National Service. Joe's travel to Canada with Mam and Dad can be seen in Joe's diary which is included in this book.

National Service

From shortly after the war, until approximately 1960-61 every male in England was required to serve in the armed forces when they reached the age of 18. Gerard was the first in our family and in his case the requirement was to serve 18 months. He went through the usual procedure, asked to go into the Royal Navy saying it was family tradition (following Uncle James and Uncle Joe). He must have been very persuasive because they allowed him to join the navy. He did his training in Devonport/Plymouth or Portsmouth, and following that was assigned to a vessel, where he did his travel. He travelled all the way around England doing anti-submarine detection (ASDIC).

He was not favourably impressed, although all the girls were – cos everybody loves a sailor , and in any case Gerard was very good-looking. One thing I do remember is that he came home one time, he had taken a train to London and was going to hitch-hike. At some stage in London he used a taxi, the fare was two & threepence, and he gave the cabbie half-a crown, to which the cabbies said "wot abaht the boy" referring to a tip. I guess he thought threepence wasn't enough, so Gerard says OK give me the threepence. He then pocketed the threepence, and said for being greedy & cheeky you get nowt!. Gerard then went to the beginning of the Great North Road (the A6), stopped at a traffic light, and kept pushing the pedestrian crossing button to stop traffic. Obviously that was a successful ploy, because he got home reasonably quickly.

Next to go was me (and obviously I have a bit more detail in my case). Received the letter, went for the medical, and as I could stand up and breathe was pronounced fit!. I also asked to go in the Navy, but unlike Gerard was told yes I could go in,------if I signed up for 12 years!! Didn't want it that badly, so was sent to the RAF, and after putting round pegs in round holes and so on was considered smart enough to go in the RAF. At the subsequent interview I was asked why I chose the RAF, to which I replied that as I couldn't get in the Navy, there were only two options left, and the RAF was the lesser of the two evils. This clearly was not the correct answer, as I was quickly told that in that case I could "Sod Off to the Army" which I did.

Following more tests I was again interviewed, this time by someone with pips on his shoulders (probably the lowest form of Officer life – a second lieutenant).He asked if I wanted to go in the Catering Corps (which to me brought visions of mountains of potatoes – and me peeling them) and I said not particularly. Next question – did I want to be in the medical corps – which brought a horrified comment that I'd rather peel spuds than have blood and bandages , This brought the final question – well what do you want to do in the Army – to which I replied – 2 years. Again not the best answer, because with a sarcastic smile he said "Oh we'll find something for you!.... and that's how I finished up in the infantry. I duly reported to Ashton under Lyne to join the Manchester Regiment, where I was asked if I wanted to go abroad, and to which I answered that I would go anywhere in the world if the King was paying. It finished up that I was the only one out of a draft of 80 not to go to Malaya – instead I finished up in Fulwood Barracks in Preston!!

While I didn't particularly want to go in the forces I guess I made the best of it and do have some pleasant memories: In Formby, which seemed to me to be a most unlikely place to train for tropical Malaya, we were housed in Quonset huts which had one small stove to heat a room for about 30 men, furthermore we were allowed ONE bucket of coal per day. It was cold! So we stole a bunch of coal, and hid it in the soldiers box at the foot of each bed , in the next hut (which was empty). When the search party looking for the stolen goods searched our hut... they didn't find it, and didn't bother with the empty hut so we did stay reasonably warm.

A somewhat similar thing happened in Fulwood barracks. A miserable one bucket of coal per room. However an "old " soldier saved the problem. New recruits came in on a Thursday (Teddie boys when they arrived) and on the Friday when they didn't quite know what they were supposed to do,Phillips (the old soldier) detailed two of them....to get that handcart, fill it with coke from the pile behind that building (which was of course the officer's mess) and dump it where I tell you (which was behind our barracks) and they like good soldiers did so!

On another occasion he suggested we cook our own supper in a dis-used kitchen suitable for cooking for 2000 men. I replied that the Quartermaster had locked the place up, but he had been there at the time and left a window open. He also produced steaks (because he had done the butcher a favour and put screens on the windows, and was able during this time to cut off some steaks (which he said wouldn't be missed) So we ate well that weekend!

The same man was caught walking down a main street in Preston with a woman of "easy virtue" who was wearing his army tunic. They were seen by an officer of a different regiment (whom she saluted and called by his first name!). The officer ordered him back to barracks.

Around 1.0' clock in the morning we were woken up by the duty officer who was looking for Phillips. We knew nothing about what had gone on and they didn't find him. The next day he was found, charged and demoted. It turns out that he had hidden in the equipment shop where he worked (and probably the woman was with him. I was quite surprised, and asked how he could possibly have got in, when he turned the shop key in to me avery night? His response: Oh No! The key I gave you was the key to my front door in Liverpool!! So much for security!

I did beat them to some degree though. When I was due for Annual leave I was entitled to a railway warrant anywhere in England. I asked for one to Dover. My boss the Major responded Dover? Dover? there's nothing at Dover but a bloody castle! I said that I liked castles, got my warrant, then went across to Europe and spent 2 weeks hitch-hiking through Belgium, Holland and France – so there!!

Next was Tom. Tom wanted to go in the Airforce, so after he joined up he was asked if he would like to serve his time (sounds like Prison doesn't it?) in the South West, South East or the North West of England. Tom immediately figured out that the only place in the North West was near Blackpool (Padgate I think) and said North West. Immediately after his training was finished he was flown not to the North West, but Far East and was in Hong Kong before he had served 2 months in the forces. He was in Hong Kong for three months and then sent to Malaya (I know its Malaysia now) where he spent the rest of his time. It was interesting to note that they flew him out there, but sailed him home via Aden and as a result he spent 10 more days than he should have.

Next and last was Neville. Neville, like Tom opted for the Air Force, and unlike Tom, spent most of his time in Gloucester. Unfortunately the only thing I remember about Neville's service was that he joined the band and played a drum (Once in a parade before the Queen Mum). I think that Neville's travel was restricted to Salford-Gloucester and return.

This is perhaps the right area to note that Mary had more travel. She had been rather close to Winnie & Bill Molloy and used to keep Winnie company when Bill worked nights (this was during the war). The Molloys emigrated to Canada in 1948, and in 1953 Mary decided that she would like to go. She did, and sailed from Liverpool and we all went to see her off (transported by Harry Marshall).

In 1958 I decided to go and visit Mary (because she was very homesick), and I thought I would stay 2 years, then go to Australia..............I haven't made it to Australia yet.

Now, to try and cover some of my Mam's travel. Her trip to Canada with Dad and Joe will be covered elsewhere. However she did lots of travel besides that. Her cousin from Australia whom Mam had corresponded with for years, made a trip to England and during her time there took Mam on a trip to Europe, one of those 17 countries in 30 days things, and I know it included Rome. Mam also went to Lourdes.

One year when we went to England, we arranged to take Mam with us on a "three capitals tour" – Amsterdam, Brussels, Paris. This was a memorable holiday for us as well as Mam. In Amsterdam the trip included a tour of the "Red Light" district, and although we tried to talk her out of it we couldn't, and as a result heard comments "They don't know what they're doing" (and a sotto voce response from another traveller saying Oh yes they do, and theyr'e doing it for money). But Mam heard that, and said "well I'll pray for them."

In Brussels the comment we liked most was when she asked Heather to "Pinch Me". "Why?" said Heather, "because I don't believe I'm really here!" In Paris the trip included a visit to the Folies Bergere, and again we couldn't dissuade her (It's part of the trip she said). Strangely enough she commented on the beautiful headdresses worn by these statuesque, near naked ladies. We realised afterwards that her eyesight had deteriorated and we simply weren't sure that she was aware of the nakedness but she was one smart lady and could well have been.

I don't recall much more about Mam's travels to Europe because of course I was in Canada at the time. Obviously, in subsequent years there was much more travel and the world seemed to be more accessible.

When I left school, I started work at a shirt manufacturers named Hogg & Mitchell. One of the perks I got was that: a) I could buy shirts cheaply, b) from time to time I would be given a shirt to "test". However, while I got the shirt for free, my Mam had to tell me how good/bad it was for washing & ironing, also had to check to see if any of the colours ran. This reminds me of another incident. You have already heard about the washing process, but not the drying! Again, no drier, our clothes were hung on a rack in the kitchen to dry. The rack had pulleys so it could be raised and lowered. One day somebody heard a passerby commenting...."That poor woman must take in washing....look at all those shirts!" I know that one day there were 37 shirts on the rack(s). At that time I used to chum around with a lot of jewish boys. One time I mentioned I was looking for a red sweater, and one of the group said (in horror) you're not going retail are you – Sammy deals in sweaters! One of the group sold fireplaces (Gerry Goodman) and for my Mam, of course, he gave her a good deal. Another one was a goldsmith who made Pauline's wedding ring and also advised Margaret on hers. A different one made a fur coat for my Mam, but told her it would take quite a while, because for her he wanted to pick the furs himself!

On a Saturday I used to meet with these friends a t Lewiss's for coffee & chocolate eclairs. There was a table reserved for us right at the front (the manageress was Jewish). And one day the waitress asked if she could take the eclairs back until the rest came............why.......... because all the other patrons were asking for them and there were no more....only ours!

Mary Emma and Ted Mather

Ted Mather

My Grandad was born 12 Jan 1875. He was a rubber spreader at Mandlebergs, and rose to be a foreman. He had many accomplishments. He was the founder and first President of St Sebastian's Working mens club. He personally was involved in making the clothing for Captain Scot'ts expedition to the Antarctic. In 1903 he was sent to Germany for Mandlebergs to help set up a new rubber factory there. He was there for about 2 years and sometime during the first world war he was sent as a diplomat to ensure that the troops were being treated properly. As a young child, I remember him telling me about visiting some kind of fairground where there was a "Wild Man of Borneo" on display, uttering weird gutteral noises in a strange tongue. My Grandad recognised it as Lancashire dialect!. and spoke to the man when nobody else was around....and was promptly asked to get lost...cos if they find out, I'll lose my job!! When war broke out in 1939 his brother in Canada (George), sent him a letter saying that a place was available for all the Mather grandchildren for the duration of the war. George also sent the same letter to all his brothers. My Grandfather never told any of his children but wrote to his brother saying: Thank you very much, but they will stay where they belong, with their families. None of us (including my Mam & Dad) knew anything about this and only found out when Neville arrived home from his first trip to Canada. Neville had been told by George's wife. At confirmation you usually have a sponsor which used to always be your father. During the second world war, when so many were in the forces, my Grandad was sponsor for EVERYONE that got confirmed the day I did! He also will be involved in many of the stories which follow.

Another thing I remember. Towards the end of his life he had some health problems (which didn't affect his somewhat mischievous mind!). A cousin of his who was a nun somewhere in the south of England wrote a letter to my Mam. She had heard that Ted Mather had passed away, and so the letter my Mam received was saying what a good man her Dad was, and praised him extensively. My Mam of course showed the letter to her Dad, who then wrote to the nun, telling her that the rumour of his death was untrue, but he was very pleased to read the kind thoughts she had about him, adding that these things are not usually heard while one is alive and he found it very gratifying!

Some of the things I remember (as a very young boy). I'd go into his house, he'd say: "Have you polished your shoes this morning?…to which of course I'd have to say "No", and then he'd tell me," Well polish them now….and while you're at it, polish mine as well." After playing football on Littleton Rd playing fields (for St Sebastian's school) I'd always call in at Number one Littleton Rd and he would want a full report of the game…. You can imagine how dirty I'd be on a wet day, (remember there were no showers then) and it didn't seem to bother him.

When he did die and we came out of church, we were very surprised to see six limos lined up outside church (which was very unusual in the 1950s). The funeral procession then went to Mandlebergs factory and all the staff were lined up to show their respects. We then realized how special he was to so many people other than us.

Perhaps here I should add that when he first came to Salford he took lodgings at the house of a man who owned a dairy, and lived at 92 Broughton Rd and subsequently married the daughter Mary Emma Walton.

A Surprise Trip to Canada from Salford Docks in 1965
by Guy Joseph Martin

PART THE FIRST
"THE SURPRISE"

In the summer of 1964, when Beatlemania was everywhere, my Dad was lucky enough to win £1,088, 10 shillings and 8 pence on (what was then called The Spastic Society) Pools. This was a very large amount of money for that time.

I am the youngest of 13 children and I knew that he had worked very hard to help bring us all up with my Mam. When I was one year old my eldest sister, Mary (named after my mother) sailed to Canada to stay with relatives for a break, from also helping to bring her younger brothers and sisters up with my Mam. She decided to stay there. Four or five years later her younger brother, Anthony, decided to visit her. I remember waving good bye to him at Liverpool Pier Head as he climbed the gangway onto the deck of the Empress of France. He also decided to stay. They both lived in Burnaby, New Westminster; about half an hour drive from Vancouver, British Columbia.

Anyway, my Dad, like all of us, missed them and wanted to see them again; having only spoken to them by phone, after the transatlantic cable had been laid from Goonhilly Downs in Cornwall. He would not travel by plane and said he would only visit them when they had built a road bridge from England to Canada so that he could ride across on his pushbike. He decided that he could cope with a sea voyage and train journey and therefore booked a passage with Furness Whithy on Manchester Liners and a three day train journey with the Canadian Pacific Railway to Vancouver.

I was very happy for them and knew that they would enjoy themselves as my Dad had arranged to take three months off work, in view of the sea and train journeys , holiday and then return home. It was with an incredible and unbelievable shock in, I think November 1964, that I was asked to sit down at the kitchen table. I thought at first that I was in trouble because those of my brothers and sisters that were in the house were stood around me. My Mam said "you can start filling this form in". I said "what is it for?", and she showed me the top of the form that explained it was for a passport. She said "you're coming to Canada with us". I was completely stunned. I completed the form with tears in my eyes for the passport (Number LO 860920) and was also shown the tickets to prove it was true. It took quite a while, for it all to sink in. It took me a very long time to fall asleep at night for a few weeks. I kept looking at the photographs that my brother Neville had taken when he went to Anthony's wedding with my sister Angela in 1961. He had brought a music box back with a statue of a moose, the tune it played was the Canadian national anthem, "Oh Canada". I used to listen to the anthem as I looked at the photographs

Over the next six months or more my Mam started to buy items of clothes and other things for my trip to Canada. A diary, 'My Trip' and a 'painting-by-numbers' set for on board ship. She also bought me a brush and comb, that I still use today, oh and I got a new suitcase, I'd never had one of those before.

In March 1965 I got my passport, Dad got the tickets and arranged for the big clothes trunk to be sent to Manchester Liners, ready to be loaded on board. I couldn't wait for the summer holidays to start. We were due to board on 5th July, our John's birthday.

But that was postponed until Sunday 1 8th July. I made my first entry in my diary. (See later). At the front of the diary were spaces to be filled in with the following titles'

My Name	Guy Joseph Martin
My Residence	47 Broughton Road, Salford 6, Lancs, England
My Telephone	PENdleton 4867

(This was when the dial on the phone had letters as well as numbers, making up the code of the area in which you lived)

The layout of the diary pages were as follows:

EVENTS AND PLACES VISITED
Date
Place
Weather

TALES OF FORTY-SEVEN

PART THE SECOND
"THE CANAL TRIP TO THE OUTWAR D JOURNEY"

We set off from 47 at about 11.00am. Dad had ordered a Black Cab. We loaded our hand luggage and all my brothers and sisters waved us off. We travelled up Broughton Road to Pendleton Church, along Broad Street and then Cross Lane to Trafford Road. We didn't go through the Dock Gates but instead down Aubrey Street to Number 9 Dock. This was the one that had the enormous reinforced concrete Grain Elevator at the end. (I didn't think that years later I would be inspecting it as a Building Control Officer, in preparation for its demolition). We drove along the dock road to Number 10 Shed passing lots of goods waiting to be loaded onto various ships, cars, large bales of cloth and cotton, large and small boxes of all sorts waiting for export. We walked through the shed and then climbed up the gangway to the deck. What struck me was the smell. Diesel, damp cloth (probably cotton) newly cut timber, oil; samples of most of these assorted objects were floating in the water alongside the ship!

I watched the sailors and stevedores stow the derricks and batten down the hatch coverings. There was a lot of activity on the decks. Then the Tug Boat arrived and towed the ship out of Number 9 Dock into the Manchester ship Canal to begin the half day trip down to Liverpool. I had been taken on a similar trip to Ellesmere Port along the Canal a few years earlier with my Mam and Dad, we took sandwiches but I didn't expect to be eating them with the backdrop of the oil, diesel and other smelly rubbish that littered the sides of the lock walls as the boat was lowered to the next level. I didn't realise that the Tug boat toilets were emptied into the Canal.

A SURPRISE TRIP TO CANADA FROM SALFORD DOCKS IN 1965

By the time we got to Barton Locks our John, having ridden by push bike, was standing on the platform at the side of the Swing Aqueduct. He had taken up photography and had built his own darkroom in the cellar of 47. He took photographs of my Mam and Dad and me as we stood on the passenger deck. I still have the photographs and used them on my return to build a replica of the Manchester Shipper, the ship that took us to Canada.

Apart from the smell the trip was very interesting, especially when we were passing through Irlam, Cadishead and Latchford with fields on each side. Occasionally people would wave to us from the banks on either side. We waved to Aunty May and Uncle Arthur at Latchford Locks and eventually arrived at Liverpool where the Tug Boat left us and we berthed for the night, waiting for the tide the next day.

My first entry in my diary is laid out below written on the Manchester Shipper. The ship was steered not by the Captain but by a Pilot, presumably employed by Manchester Liners, who's duty it was to direct the crew in negotiating the locks and channels of the Manchester Ship Canal to Liverpool.

I have realised in looking at my diary after nearly forty years, just how bad my spelling and grammar was. I wrote most of the entries as one long sentence, but to make it easier to understand I have now inserted the necessary commas and full stops. I have also included (in parenthesis) corrections made by my mother. I haven't tried to change the style or way that a thirteen year old looked at the world. I think it is important to re-visit Canada through the eyes of a thirteen year old in 1965, I think it has a special feel.

EVENTS AND PLACES VISITED	
Date	18 Jul 1965
Place	Salford 6
Weather	Nice day for sailing

I felt scared going on the Boat knowing that I would have to do lifeboat practise. We left Salford Docks 1.35pm. I was on the deck most of the day. In the evening we saw Aunty May and Uncle Arthur on Latchford Locks.
133 Miles at 14.00 Miles per hour.

PART THE THIRD
"SAILING OUT TO SEA"

It's one thing being pulled down the Manchester Ship Canal by a Tug and a completely different thing sailing under your own steam out at sea When sailors have said, 'beware of the currents' I hadn't realised fully what they meant. I soon found out. Ferries have a relatively flat hull, whereas ships hulls are shaped from the pointed prow or 'beak' in a 'V' sloping gradually to a Wide 'U' to the rear of the vessel. Unless the weather is a bit rough ferries sail quite smoothly. Ships, on the other hand, are designed to plough the waves. When we left the Mersey Basin and entered the Irish Sea tide, currents and wind combined to force the crew to work hard to keep the ship on the right course. People have spoken about bobbing about on the sea but to steer a cargo ship fully laden, cutting across currents and wind is a skilful exercise. The ship not only pitches forward and tosses backwards, it also rolls from side to side. Both of these movements combine out at sea I was told by Captain Askew, rough as the Irish Sea is, that the

A SURPRISE TRIP TO CANADA FROM SALFORD DOCKS IN 1965

Atlantic is much worse. It seems the general rule is that the ship starts off fairly smoothly on the first wave and gradually increases pitch, usually up to the final seventh wave, when it starts abruptly once again. The ship moves forward but with a combined pitch and roll. When standing on the bridge the bow of the ship moves in a low elipse from side to side, whilst at the same time moving forward.

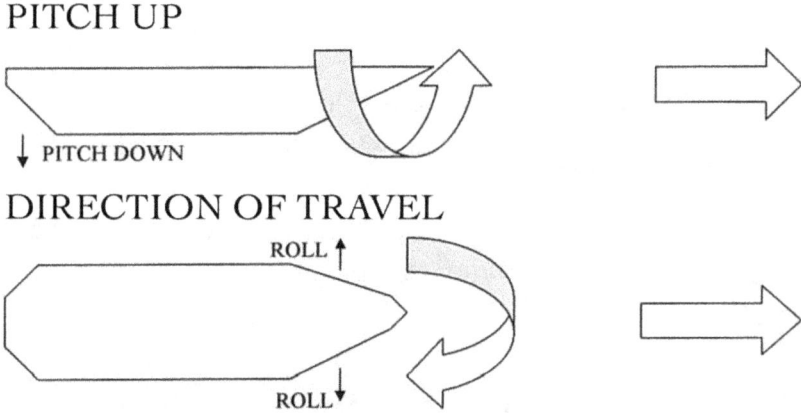

We sailed past the Isle of Man, past Giants Causeway around the northern point of Malin Head and out to sea. The initial change in movement that we experienced sailing out of the Mersey Basin into the Irish Sea was multiplied about three times as we entered the waters of the Atlantic. We hit the Gulf Stream and immediately began the pitching and tossing/rolling dance. The weather was fairly good but there were also plenty of small 'white horses' where the waves crashed in the light breeze, spitting out lots of foam.

Next diary entry:

TALES OF FORTY-SEVEN

EVENTS AND PLACES VISITED	
Date	19th July 1965
Place	Out in the open sea
Weather	Lovely sunny day
Mam was out all day on the Deck knitting I was playing Shuffleboard with the Captain's wife, first half I won, second half she won. Towards the afternoon we had lifejacket practice. I felt scared knowing that I might have to use it.	

My cabin was on the starboard side, portholes facing north on the outward journey. I don't know if this is true but I have been told that P.O.S.H. stands for Portside Outward Starboard Homeward. This is so that the rich people could always catch the sun when sailing to and from the United States of America and Canada.

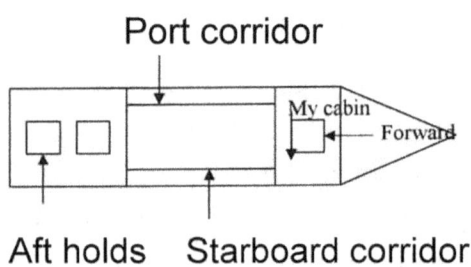

The bunk lay fore and aft against the starboard bulkhead, beneath the portholes. The chest of drawers were opposite the bunk and at its foot was the wardrobe. Between the wardrobe and the door there was a desk. I also had an easy chair for reading.

My lifejacket was on the top of the wardrobe but after life-jacket practice I placed it at the foot of the bunk. Each day

A SURPRISE TRIP TO CANADA FROM SALFORD DOCKS IN 1965

when the steward had been in my room to clean he put it back on the top of the wardrobe, and when I came in the first thing I did was to put it back on the bunk. He eventually persuaded me that if there was an emergency I would have plenty of time to get it off the top of the wardrobe, so I relented.

The first night in bed I found it very difficult to get to sleep. I kept rolling from side to side and could feel my bodyweight moving from my feet to my head. This started off slow and gentle then gradually increased to the crescendo of the seventh wave, where the whole process started again. I explained to the steward how difficult it was for me to get off to sleep and he told me that most sailors had the same problem. He explained how they got over it, by taking their kit bag and placing it inside the bunk leaving a gap between the kit bag and the bulkhead for you to sleep in. I didn't have a kit bag so he got my suitcase and used that instead. That night I got to sleep straight away, and every night afterwards.

One difficulty we all had was walking around the ship. It was first and foremost a cargo ship but had room for twelve passengers. Most passengers were millionaires who were accompanying their exports that were stowed in the hold of the ship. The passenger deck was positioned beneath the lounge which was beneath the bridge. The forward most room was the dining room with cabins either side. Outside and in the middle of the ship facing forward was the staircase leading to the lounge. This was separated from the remaining cabins by a corridor running 'athwart ships' from side-to-side. There were two corridors running parallel fore and aft with cabins either side. These corridors terminated aft at the Galley. Beyond this at a lower level were the rear holds.

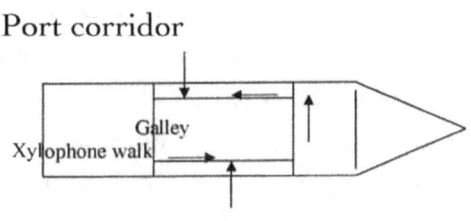

Mealtimes were announced by one of the stewards who would play a tune on a three note xylophone walking from the Galley forward up the starboard side corridor past the dining room doors and then aft down the port side corridor. I was quickly asked to take over this job to keep me occupied. The two long corridors were about 1.2Metres wide and the trick was to walk the centre throwing your weight forward/left and then rear/right so that you didn't crash into the bulkhead (corridor walls). This was known as 'getting your sea legs'

Next diary entry:

EVENTS AND PLACES VISITED	
Date	21st July 1965
Place	Out in the open sea
Weather	Rather cold and wind
Mam sat on the deck in the morning knitting, as usual. I was 'painting-by-numbers' in the lounge, then at night it got rough so we had a cartoon, then after that we had a mad film called 'Bye Bye Birdie'.	

A SURPRISE TRIP TO CANADA FROM SALFORD DOCKS IN 1965

The film was shown in the dining room. The steward set up the reel to reel projector on one of the tables and a large white bed sheet was pinned to one of the beams supporting the ceiling. As it says in the diary the sea was rough with the ship pitching, tossing and rolling. This caused the sheet to slide and fold from side to side and backwards and forwards. That meant the film kept getting blurred. At least it took your mind off the rough sea for a while.

When we sat down for the evening meal the sea was still rough. The stewards brought soup for the starter. We were sat, as usual, at the Captain's table. When you are on land eating soup is very easy. You have to tilt the soup bowl, slide the spoon in and eat. At sea I forgot how the table is fixed to the floor and moves with the ship. In the galley the hob is fixed on two axles, just like the compass on the monkey island on the poop deck. They are oriented fore and aft and athwart ships, this keeps the oil, fat, pans and boiling water level all the time no matter what the ship does. So I tilted my soup bowl, looked up to talk to my mother, and then felt the hot soup on my lap and then dribbling down my legs, much to the amusement of those at our table.

I noticed that several sailors were on the forward deck putting tarpaulin sheets over the holds. They were hammering wedges very tightly to keep them in place. They were also fixing steel bars with hooks onto the derricks. I asked one of the crew what they were doing and he said "battening down the hatches because we are expecting bad weather".

Whilst I was on the bridge one trick that I used to play was holding onto the catches that held the window shut. Facing the bows and watching the waves and spindrift blowing right over the ship from the starboard side to the port side without hitting the deck. If I held on tight enough I could stay vertical to the window and lean from side to side with the ship instead of leaning the opposite way to stop myself from falling over. The Captain got very amused by this. He would take the opportunity to tell me stories of things that had happened to him out at sea.

One thing that I did not realise was that we would lose one hour every day. The result of this was that, in effect, I woke up earlier and earlier each day. This waking up earlier was compounded by the wonderful smell of toast. I opened the cabin door, after hearing the steward knock, and found a cup of tea and two pieces of buttered toast. It's great being at sea!!

Next diary entry:

EVENTS AND PLACES VISITED	
Date	22nd July 1965
Place	Out on the open sea
Weather	Very rough indeed?
The boat was Rocking and Rolling and tipping. The water was splashing over the forward deck, really it was great. The weather was rough because we were on the edge of an anticyclone. My Mam was knitting in the lounge all day but in the morning when the steward came in he put coffee on the table , then it started to fall off so she grabbed, it went, chair and all, at dinner all the cutlery slid off the tables, we also had soup.	

Anyway while I was on the bridge with him I noticed that three separate sailors had spoken to him within five minutes of one another about an incident that had happened on the forward deck. Next thing he asked me to go with him where he met my mother near the dining room just as she was coming back inside from the passenger deck. He stopped her and asked her why she had gone down the companion stairs onto the forward deck, past the holds, when the waves were breaking over the side. He was quite annoyed and said "do you know that three of my crew have reported that you were on the forward deck, in very dangerous conditions and that you could have been injured, or worse, even killed. Now please don't go out there again until either I or a member of the crew tell you it's safe to do so. The safest place for you is inside and not on the deck".

As the sea was getting more rough and after my soup episode at dinner, the steward made some adjustments to the table. He raised the edges, by about two inches and locked them in place, known as a fiddle. He then splashed water on the table cloths. This was to stop the cutlery and plates from sliding off the table. The Captain also pointed out that the condiment jars all had flat and wide bases to stop them from falling over.

That night I had a lot of trouble trying to get to sleep because of the wind and rain but mostly because of the wire coat hangers in the wardrobe. They were sliding from one side to the other and banging together with the roll of the ship. I had to put my waste bin in the wardrobe as it kept rolling around the floor and making a noise. Worst of all was the fact that my cabin was next to the dining room. The cutlery in the drawers had a dance with the plates in their racks, and the pans on their hooks sliding one way and then the other crashing in their drawers and containers.

For a whole day, after passing the anticyclone, I was on deck in the sun and asked the chief engineer, who was doing his daily walk around the ship after lunch, what the intermittent loud rattling noise was. He explained that it was the rudder and that we were only travelling half speed because of the swells. The ocean was calming down after the anticyclone and, whilst there were no waves breaking, the surface was moving alternately up and down without splashing. The distance from the peak to the trough was about forty feet. Because of this the ship alternates from having a peak fore and aft with a trough amidships, to peak amidships and trough fore and aft. When the latter happens the propeller is out of the sea spinning in the air, that's what you can hear echoing off the swells. Isn't life exciting at sea?

I only had a cup of coffee once. It was a mixture of hot coffee and hot milk. It was the only time I felt sick, and not because of the rough sea.

Next diary entry:

EVENTS AND PLACES VISITED	
Date	23rd July 1965
Place	Same again
Weather	Misty all day and most of the night
The fog signal was going all day, at intervals, and most of the night. I slept well in spite of it. The fog signal is the ship's hooter, it hoots for at least one minute then waits five minutes, then does it again.	

Its funny how the sound of the fog-horn echoed back in the fog. It made it sound very loud.

Next diary entry:

A SURPRISE TRIP TO CANADA FROM SALFORD DOCKS IN 1965

EVENTS AND PLACES VISITED
Date   24th July 1965
Place   Same again
Weather Lovel sunny day
My Mam got bumt by the sun on the arms and on the lips, her lips were the worst, they had a scab on for a few days after. The Captain allowed us on the bridge to see a school of whales. We passed Belle Isle and went into the straits. The Manchester Spinner's radar broke down so it held her up. The Shipper passed her. Mam started my pullover.

It was around this period that I was allowed on the bridge again by the Captain who let me look through his huge sea binoculars. I was looking at the Manchester Spinner and Commercial and also a school of whales blowing water through their spouts.

Mam made matching pullovers for me and my Dad and a cardigan for herself to wear on deck.

Next diary entry:

EVENTS AND PLACES VISITED
Date   25th July 1965
Place   Passed Belle Isle in the strait
Weather   Ran into mist
We ran into mist. The Spinner passed us in the morning, later it started to rain so we can't go out. Ted tied a fishes head to Pats tap. She screamed then Vick went in and came out quick screaming at the same time. Sorry my mistake but Ted put fish in Pats room on 26th not 25th

177

Next diary entry:

EVENTS AND PLACES VISITED
Date   26th Jul 1965
Place   St Lawrence neared
Weather   Good
It is Mrs Askew's birthday today. My Mam finished my pullover. It is a bit chilly today. The first Pilot has come aboard. We celebrated Mrs Askew's birthday in the lounge with a cocktail party. Ted put fish in Pats room. It thundered once and my Mam saw reflection of a rainbow in the sea.

There were several pilots for the St Lawrence Seaway and Lake Ontario, they used to come aboard up a companion ladder let down at the side of the ship. The Saint Lawrence Seaway varies in width from about the same width as the Manchester Ship Canal (wide enough for two Liners to pass each other) to very wide indeed. We spent two days being tugged down the seaway passing small islands with very expensive houses on. There were lots of small craft, sailing boats and motorboats coming right up to the side of our ship so that the people on board could say hello and wave to us.

Just before we entered Lake Ontario we passed through the "Thousand Islands". These are lots of islands of varying sizes each with their own jetties with very expensive houses and yachts moored alongside. I have never seen the display of so much money concentrated in one place before.

PART THE FOURTH
"TORONTO AND EASTERN RELATIVES"

Next diary entry:

EVENTS AND PLACES VISITED	
Date	29th July 1965
Place	242 Herbert Street, Kitchener, Waterloo
Weather	Very hot weather
I was at Aunty Dorothy's and with Michael, Monica, Peter and Rosemary (Bird). I tried to catch a squirrel. The squirrel went in the trap but came right out, then a bird went in and Peter caught it when we were all inside eating dinner.	

One day when we went to Kitchener centre to do some shopping I encountered a family of Mennonites. They are of Dutch origin who follow a similar lifestyle to the Amish. They do not have or use modern machinery and travel by horse and buggy. They wear black clothes, the older men usually have long beards and they don't like you to take their photograph.

While I was staying at Aunty Dorothy Bird's I helped her son Michael with his paper round. We walked all around the district with Michael saying hello to his friends. I also remember collecting empty fizzy drink bottles and taking them back to the shop to collect a dime for each. This was also the first time I had seen a skateboard. I tried riding one but kept falling off as it went too fast and I couldn't control it.

Funnily enough when I got back to England one of the first things I did was to dismantle one of my sister's metal roller skates in half. I cut myself and shaped a short piece of plywood and screwed the heal part to the rear and the toe part to the front to create my own skateboard. I suspect that this was one of the first skateboards in England. I used to skate down London Street in Salford, much to the nonplussed look on the faces of people passing by.

I remember Michael taking me to a baseball match but I could not get quite as excited about it as he did. I got very bored. I just thought of it as a game of rounders played with larger bats. I tried to explain cricket to him but he just couldn't get the hang of it. I didn't find it as interesting or exciting as football.

Next diary entry:

EVENTS AND PLACES VISITED	
Date	1st August 1965
Place	Bellwood
Weather	Pretty good
We went to Bellwood, Aunty Ada's cottage. I went there in the morning but towards the afternoon all the relations to the Mathers' came and they had their own food with them so I had tea with the Bird's. We went to St Joseph's Church.	

Bellwood was the weekend cottage of Ada and Lou Beaupre, Ada was a cousin of my mother. My mother first went to Canada for two years when she was eighteen, she stayed with Ada and also went to work with her.

The Mather gathering at Bellwood was an annual event. Each family brought their own food and there were several stone barbecue hearths scattered around the cottage close to the shore. This was the first time I had a barbecued banana. They wrapped it in tinfoil and placed it in the hot coals. When steam could be seen coming out of the tinfoil it was ready and was placed in a bowl to be eaten with ice cream. It was very good. It is also now a favourite of my children.

Next diary entry:

EVENTS AND PLACES VISITED	
Date	7th August 1965
Place	Cottage at Bellwood
Weather	Very good indeed
We were there for a week. My Dad and I was painting the cottage with Uncle Lou. Aunty Gloria and Uncle Harvey. Uncle Lou, Uncle Harvey and my Dad was painting the walls of the cottage while Gloria and I were painting the tables and chairs in the garden. Aunty Ada was in watching TV, my Mam was knitting, as usual! !	

Bellwood was a very relaxing place to be. Harvey showed me what the 'Stinker' was for. He went to the lake and caught a couple of fish, cut their heads off and placed them in a specially shaped glass jar that had an aluminium cone shaped lid. He then hung it up under the porch roof near the door. He explained that all the mosquitoes and flies smelt the rotting fish heads and made their way into the jar. The lid was shaped in such a way that they could get in but could not get out. When the jar was full of dead flies it was emptied on the fire and more fish were caught to continue the process. This, hopefully, kept the mosquitoes and flies out of the property.

The only thing I didn't like about the cottage was the toilet. It consisted of an earth closet with a simple wooden board to sit on. It was the worst smell I had ever experience, especially when Lou topped it up with neat lime to clean it.

Next diary entry:

EVENTS AND PLACES VISITED
Date   8th August 1965
Place   Bellwood Cottage
Weather Very good and sunny
Today is my Mam and Dad's anniversary of 37 years marriage. It was a lovely dinner cooked by Gloria Uncle Harvey and Lou were working on the horse shoe pitch. My Mam had a ride in Aunty Ada's motorboat.

My Mam and Dad had a really great time, everyone was pleased for them and made sure that their day went well.

When we were at the cottage Harvey showed me and my Dad how to play horseshoes. They had Canadian ones which are a large version of a real horseshoe. They have two steel pegs set in a 1.3M square sand pit positioned about 6m apart. Staring at one of the sand pits the idea is to get the three horseshoes around the peg. The American horseshoes are larger than the Canadian ones and they are more of a square shape with a metal lug facing inwards at the end of the straight legs, this makes it more likely to hook around the peg.

Next diary entry:

A SURPRISE TRIP TO CANADA FROM SALFORD DOCKS IN 1965

I don't know why I wrote '7 of Hearts', maybe that was a winning card for me.

Although there is no diary entry, it was around this time that Lou took us to see Niagara Falls. The weather was very sunny and as we approached the viewing platform the noise of the water falling over the edge got louder and louder. The mist hung in the air over the pool, covering the sightseeing boat "Maid of the Mist". We could also see visitors in yellow raincoats walking down and behind the waterfall from the Canadian side to the American side. We stayed there quite a long time and had something to eat in a restaurant.

Next diary entry:

In this area of Canada all foodstuff packets such as cornflakes and jam etc had both English and French writing on them. There were quite a few French cartoons on TV as well.

It was around this time that I was taken to a Drive-in Cinema. The screen was positioned in the comer of the plot and car spaces were marked out in a slight curve, all facing the screen of course, with posts on each side of the front doors to the car. The driver and front passenger then wound their windows down and positioned a small speaker, on a flexible cable, inside the car. They then hung it on the inside of the window and then wound the window back up, in case it rained. After the film a team of marshals organised the safe exit of all the cars, row by row

Next diary entry:

EVENTS AND PLACES VISITED	
Date	11th August 1965
Place	Cottage Bellwood
Weather	Very hot and sunny
We were painting all day at the cottage. We all had to go to bed early because we were going to Jacksons Point.	

I've just realised how Ada and Lou took advantage of us being there to maintain their holiday home!

Next diary entry:

EVENTS AND PLACES VISITED	
Date	12th August 1965
Place	Jacksons Point
Weather	Very good
We went to Jacksons Point to see Uncle Neville. We all had a lovely day at the De La Salle Boys Camp. Each set of boys was named after Indians and each set of Indians had their own Totem Poles. Mam, Dad, Lou, Ada, Harvey and Gloria went to town and on the way back the car broke down. After a bit they found out they needed a new starter.	

Uncle Neville, Ada's brother, was a Brother of the De La Salle Christian Brothers, the Order was formed by John Baptiste De La Salle. Uncle Neville taught the boys at the nearby school. Some of my older brothers, Uncles' and I went to the De La Salle Grammar school in Weaste Lane Salford.

A SURPRISE TRIP TO CANADA FROM SALFORD DOCKS IN 1965

Next diary entry

EVENTS AND PLACES VISITED	
Date	14th August 1965
Place	Bellwood Cottage
Weather	Very sunny
We were ready to say good bye to Bellwood. Our friends came to say good bye to us. Friends of Aunty Ada and Uncle Lou came to take over for a week. Elmer and Brian Sherman took us on a trip up and down the lake in his motor boat. Elmer let me steer the boat, then on the way off the boat my Mam nearly fell in and Elmer got the bottom of his pants wet.	

I pulled the throttle back, speeded up and did a few quick turns left and right so fast that water nearly came into the bottom of the boat. Pretty soon Elmer took over the controls again.

My Mam's experience should have been cought on film. She stood up, was supported by Dad and Elmer and got one leg out of the boat. As she tried to get the other leg out and on to the jetty the boat started to move away into the lake. She just started to laugh of course and fortunately my Dad and Elmer managed to get her ashore.

Next diary entry:

EVENTS AND PLACES VISITED	
Date	16th August 1965
Place	Waterloo
Weather	Had been raining all night
We went to the CPR to collect our tickets to Coquitlam. We called at the Beaupre's Store. On the way home Lou took us on a tour of all the wonderful pretty houses in Waterloo and to see the University buildings. We leave Waterloo tomorrow.	

Lou explained that these houses looked like solid brickwork but in fact were timber framed with brickwork only on the outside. They were built in the typical New England style.

PART THE FIFTH
"THE OUTWARD TRAIN JOURNEY"

Next diary entry:

EVENTS AND PLACES VISITED	
Date	17th August 1965
Place	Kitchener CPR station
Weather	Fair
Lou and Ada took us to Kitchener CPR railway station. We left at 2.35pm and arrived at Toronto at 3.55pm. We left Toronto at 6.10pm. We had dinner at 7.00pm on the Canadian Pacific Railway train then sat in the dome until 10.00pm.	

The trains were very long, not like the ones in England. They had two engines at the front pulling twenty seven

A SURPRISE TRIP TO CANADA FROM SALFORD DOCKS IN 1965

carriages (or cars, as they call them). They had a dome car in the middle and a dome car at the end, the end dome car tapered to the rear with a glass door so that you could see the track, mountains and countryside you were leaving behind.

Next diary entry

EVENTS AND PLACES VISITED	
Date	18th August 1965
Place	The train
Weather	Very good all the way
We got up at 7.30am not knowing that we could have gone to breakfast right away, but anyway we sat in our cabin till 9.00 0'clock am, then we asked a Porter about breakfast. He told us to go there so we did. After breakfast we stopped at Schrieber 5 mins. We stopped at Fort William 15mins. We got out and had a walk. They served very good meals on the train all the way there.	

I remember having the finest Spanish Omelette that I have ever tasted. We were in a car just behind the middle dome car. I met a boy about my age who was in a car not far from the end. We used to get together to play cards and other games. Anyway when we got to Winnipeg (the halfway stage where the train and engines had a major overhaul) we stopped for about one and a half hours. I was in his car when we arrived and after a while I said I'd have to get back to my Mam and Dad. I thought I'd walk along outside the train but when I'd passed a few cars I stood still, horrified. The front half of the train, with my Mam and Dad in it, was missing. I started to feel sick at the thought of them going on without me and that I'd be left in Winnipeg to wait for an engine. I went up to the nearest Guard and asked him where the front part of the train was. He looked at the worried expression on my face and with a smile said: "Why its right here on the next track son. We split the train in half at Winnipeg so that we don't have to walk too far to service it". I then had to walk *back* to get to our car.

Next diary entry:

EVENTS AND PLACES VISITED	
Date	Same date
Place	Same place
Weather	Same weather
Trees Trees Trees and yet more Trees with a few houses-here-and-there. Plains and on them cowboys. Passed Calgary, Banff. Through the Rockies, passed Glacier National Park.	

One curious thing that my Dad found out about our very compact compartment was that there was a small cupboard next to the door with "shoes" written on it. He said "that's handy, I suppose it's so that they don't get in the way when the beds have been put down at night time" In the morning, however, when he opened the cupboard to retrieve them, he found that they had been cleaned. This was the job of the Car Porter who was in the compartment at the end of our car. Another of his jobs, after telling us when dinner was ready and in our absence, was to pull down the two bunk beds from the side wall, one on top of the other. My Mam and Dad had very comfortable sleeps but I was consigned to the reclining chair, that did not fully recline to a horizontal position. I ended up with a bit of a stiff neck.

Another job of the Car Porter was to place the portable steps outside the car door when the train stopped at stations along the route. He would stand there helping people on and off the train. When the train was about to leave the station he would shout in a loud singing voice "All aboard", 'All-a'- would slide down to a low note to be followed by a quickly rising 'board'. I used to enjoy listening to him and always think of him when I sing Chatenooga Choo Choo.

A few years ago my brother Anthony sent me a 'History Channel video' he had seen advertised by the Canadian Pacific Railway Company that had been used in the fifties and sixties to promote their train journeys. It took the train trip from East to West Canada stopping at selected CPR Hotels and right the way over to Vancouver Island by way of the ferries. It was quite nostalgic, but very dated as everybody is smiling to one another all the time with very strange and seriously dodgy bouncy sixties music in the background.

Next diary entry:

EVENTS AND PLACES VISITED	
Date	19 August 1965
Place	Rockies
Weather	Same
I'm so excited I am really in the Rockies now. I keep running from side to side of the train looking at the big hills. (Mam wrote "mountains")	

One thing that I did quite often was to stand in the link section between the cars. There were moveable plates on the floor to enable you to walk through the train whilst it was negotiating long curved bends. In here I could smell the dust wafting in through the moveable floor mixed with the smell of pine trees and woodsmoke. Back in our compartment I looked out of the window but couldn't see the top of the mountains because the sides were so steep and the track was as close as possible to the rock face without being dangerous. I had to lie on the floor close up to the window and could just about see the top of the mountains.

There were three main events that stood out on the train journey. The first was the spiral tunnels at Kicking Horse Pass. We entered the sequence at high level on the very steeply sided mountain. The train reduced speed to about five or ten miles an hour. It then started to turn, with the curve of the mountain, and began rolling gently from side to side tilting into the curve as it went. I looked down the side of the mountain and could see a railway track about two or three hundred feet below me. The train spiralled down inside the mountain as the wheels screeched and screeched on the rails, the cars rolling gently. We then came out into the open and across a short bridge into the other mountain and turned the opposite way. The same screeching and rolling. We eventually came out onto the track that I had seen from two or three hundred feet higher.

The second was emerging from the 5 mile long Connought Tunnel in the Selkirk Mountains to cross the single track 148M long Stoney Creek Bridge. It spanned the biggest ravine I had ever seen. It left one side and ventured out into what I felt was the unknown. We travelled away from the rock face as we could see the thin waterfall in the middle of the ravine. The bridge supports went half way down the mountain and spanned out across the gap and met in the middle. The train had to travel at two miles and hour so that it didn't cause dangerous oscillating vibrations. Because we were travelling so slow it felt like an age to get over. It was a fabulous view though.

The third was when we passed Hell's Mouth along the Simon Frazer River. This was where the River dropped down over large concrete platforms. We could see the salmon jumping up them to the higher levels to reach the exit to the Pacific Ocean. Not far away from this is a statue to Simon Frazer who navigated the River from inland as he tried to prove that it exited in the Pacific Ocean. He gave up at this point where his statue stands. It says on the inscription that if he had dipped his finger in the water he would probably have tasted ocean salt water and carried on.

PART THE SIXTH
"BRITISH COLUMBIA AND WESTERN RELATIVES"

Next diary entry:

EVENTS AND PLACES VISITED	
Date	20th August 1965
Place	Coquitlam
Weather	Raining lightly
We arrived at New Westminster. Bill, Mary and children, Anthony, Heather and Wendy met us at the station. Joe was surprised at how young Mam and Dad looked and found out later how fit they were. Bill Winnie and Angela called to see us in the evening.	

Apart from the summer months British Columbia is much like Manchester. We got off the train to be greeted by a Manchester downpour, and our relatives. The strange thing was that my nephews and nieces were wearing Mandleberg raincoats. They just looked like someone from home. The Mandleberg factory manufactured water proof materials, such as raincoats, and was located between Broughton Road and Seaford Road in Salford. My grandDad, Ted Mather, was a foreman or manager there when they waterproofed the tents that Captain Scott used for his fateful Antarctic adventure.

Next diary entry:

EVENTS AND PLACES VISITED	
Date	21st August 1965
Place	PNE
Weather	Nice hot sunny day
We went to see the PNE (Pacific National Exhibition) in town. I got very little of the parade on the film because of the stupid camera. It would not work properly. At night time we went to Aunty Winnies to see Uncle Billy's films.	

Uncle Bill is unique, he talks a lot (just like me) but all about Canada and how good he is. It's a good job that he is funny with it. For example, when we went up Mount Baker and Anthony was taking a photograph of us all, with the 10,000 ft mountain in the background he said, "Bill, can you just bend your head a bit so that I can get the mountain in as well?". We all had a good laugh

Next diary entry:

EVENTS AND PLACES VISITED	
Date	22nd August 1965
Place	New Westminster
Weather	I went to lacrosse with Angela and Wayne. We went to Mass with Anthony, stayed at his place for breakfast and lunch. Mam and Dad went on a tour of New Westminster and Vancouver.	

Lacrosse is a very tough, physical game. The ball is flung through the air very fast and can cause damage to people, as in the case of Wayne who had lost a couple of teeth as a result of being hit.

While I was in New Westminster I used to get bottles of Mountain Dew and 7UP. They were such refreshing drinks in the hot weather. I used to go to the nearest corner store. I remember one day, as I was walking to the store I heard a terrific noise, screeching of brakes and a big thump. I had witnessed a car accident on the corner of two streets. I remember a big row breaking out between the two drivers, just before the Police arrived. I also used to buy Chicklets and Lifesavers (different flavours of Polo mints). This was because our Mary used to send parcels from Canada every now and then with presents for us all at 47. She used to include sketches she had done of Indians and other Canadian topics. Best of all I liked the Chicklets because they tasted of Cinnamon.

Next diary entry:

EVENTS AND PLACES VISITED	
Date	25th August 1965
Place	Squamish
Weather	Dull in the mountains
Uncle Bill took us to Squamish. After that we went on to Lake Alice. Unfortunately Bill took the wrong turning and we went to some place way out in the wilds. Anyway we finally went to Allouette Lake. After that we went to dinner at the Caribou Trail Motel. We went shopping with Mary, Joe and family.	

When Bill drove his car in the wrong direction we ended up on the side of a mountain, on a single track gravel mountain road that was really only for logging trucks. As we turned comers etc the wheels skidded. I got quite frightened as I was looking out of the window right next to the edge of the road to see the river hundreds of feet below. Eventually he found a place where he could turn round.

I used to buy embroidered coat badges of all the places I visited, including Squamish. I still have them somewhere in a box.

Next diary entry:

A SURPRISE TRIP TO CANADA FROM SALFORD DOCKS IN 1965

EVENTS AND PLACES VISITED
Date   27th August 1965
Place   PNE grounds
Weather   Very good indeed
We went to the PNE fair ground. It was the first time I had ever been on and driven a GO-KART, it really was great. We left at 11.45pm. It was a marvellous exhibition. We should have gone earlier because we missed lots of things. SAT. Went to Fort Langley Historical place, saw arrowheads found on Strawberry Hill Mr Sharp. It was a glorious day.

I still have the arrowheads and enjoyed the experience of touching and sitting in chairs and walking along the battlements on the Fort walls, smelling the sun bleached timbers of the palings scored with arrow marks.

Next diary entry:

EVENTS AND PLACES VISITED
Date   29th August 1965 (Sunday)
Place   Mission City
Weather   Very good
We went to Mission City with Mary, Joe, Angela, Anthony, Peter, Stella and Paul. We also went to The Poor Clare's for Benediction, then to Westminster Abbey, Christ the King Seminary, then we went to Storeyland on the way home.

I took some very stupid photographs of a black cow. Why? I don't know!!

Next diary entry:

EVENTS AND PLACES VISITED
Date   30th August 1965
Place   Portland USA
Weather   Very good for a long trip
We left Mary's at 9.30 am for Portland. We called at the bank m Vancouver. We left Vancouver at 10.05am. We arrived in Portland and stayed at the Knickerbocker Motel at 6.30pm. 341 Miles from Mary's to Portland. We are going in for supper tonight. (Mam's writing) Had supper at the Lloyd Centre.

On the way to Portland we stayed halfway into Oregon at The Cariboo Trail Motel. It was a very nice meal and the waiter was Chinese. We all looked at the menu to decide what we would have but my Dad did not have his glasses with him. As usual he started to have a bit of a laugh and when the waiter arrived to take the order, without thinking he said "I'm sorry but this is all chinese to me!" We all looked at one another, and then to the waiter who just laughed. My Dad didn't have a clue what he had said.

We went through the centre of Seattle and we saw the 'needle', a large tapering tower with a revolving restaurant at the top. We then continued through the Rockies following the Gold Prospectors Cariboo Trail. At times the roadway got very narrow through the mountains with a very steep drop down to the river.

A SURPRISE TRIP TO CANADA FROM SALFORD DOCKS IN 1965

On the way down to Portland we stopped off at the side of the highway where foresters had cut down a large Sequoia's tree or Great Redwood. They had placed a log of about 25 ft long by about 15 ft diameter on its side and had hollowed it out, put in a door and window to create a "log" trailer or motor home. Next to it was the bottom part, probably of the same tree, stood upright but with the bottom, central part, removed to allow visitors to drive through. I took a photograph of our Anthony's car driving through it.

Next diary entry:

EVENTS AND PLACES VISITED	
Date	Thursday 31st August '65
Place	Shrine of the Sorrowful Mother
Weather	Nice hot sunny day
We went to The Shrine of The Sorrowful Mother today. It is a beautiful place. We went to the Lloyd Shopping Centre. We had a tour of Portland as well. 77 Miles. A lot of boats and water skiers were on the Jantsan Beach. 118.5 setting out 359 Miles. We left the USA for Vancouver Island and on the way called at Seattle Zoo to see two big Gorillas.	

I had taken a Kodak Box Camera with me that was given to me by my brother Gerard. I had black and white films with me but when we went to Portland I had brought a colour film. I took a long manual exposure of 6 seconds inside the Church of The Sorrowful Mother. I also remember going up to the organist and requesting him to play Clare De Lune as we walked around the grounds. Now every time I hear the tune I automatically think of that day and the peaceful gardens.

When we were at a checkout in the Lloyd Centre the checkout girl asked if we were from England, because of our accents. She asked me whereabouts and in a thick northern accent I said 'Manchisto'. She laughed and said 'What a cute accent, is that near Liverpool?' and I said 'yes'. She replied 'Do you know the Beatles?' Oh if only dear Miss, not knowing that in 1999 at my daughter Sarah's Graduation I would meet and talk to Paul McCartney.

Next diary entry:

EVENTS AND PLACES VISITED	
Date	1st September 1965
Place	Victoria Vancouver Island
Weather	Breezy but good
Victoria at the start, mile outer was 477 Miles. 135 Miles to day from Vancouver Island to New Westminster. We saw Butchart Gardens, we also had a trip round the Island. We went over the ferry. We saw lots of Abitus trees and we stopped at the Admiral Motel (Mam's writing) in Victoria.	

Butchart Gardens was superb. The gardens had been constructed in a disused quarry.

A vast derelict valley. There were different themes of garden from Japanese to English Country Garden. They had a vast army of gardeners and specialist equipment to keep the gardens in first class condition. One of the pieces of equipment was a small watering tractor. It was about 300mm wide and 60()mm long. It had two large wheels at the back and two small wheels at the front that spanned either side of the hose pipe

A SURPRISE TRIP TO CANADA FROM SALFORD DOCKS IN 1965

that fitted on the tractor. Powered by the water pressure the tractor first moved forward spraying water over the lawn on which it had been placed, and then when it reached the end of the hosepipe it automatically went backwards to carry out the whole process again. I thought it was a fantastic device.

Next diary entry:

EVENTS AND PLACES VISITED	
Date	2nd September 1965
Place	Vancouver Island Nanaimo
Weather	Lovely Sun set
We left Vancouver Island by way of Duncan and Nanaimo for New Westminster. We called at a friend of Heather on the way off Vancouver Island. Wendy and Dave Reed. We left on the Queen of Nanaimo ferry. We stopped at Julia's and met Walter and got some Halibut for Mary, he had caught it that day, and then stayed at Anthony's the night.	

I remember that at some time while we were on Vancouver Island, I think when we were visiting Julia's, I trod on a grass snake. It scared me to death until I found out that they were all over the place and were not harmful.

Next diary entry:

EVENTS AND PLACES VISITED	
Date	3rd September 1965
Place	New Westminster
Weather	The weather was very good
We came back to Mary's by way of Vancouver Town Anthony and Heather went to pick Wendy up, who had stayed at Patricia's while we went to Portland. We stayed at home and wrote out some cards and letters to people in England. When we came home and had some films and cartoons at Mary's.	

One extraordinary event that took place while I was staying at our Mary's was the work that was place on a house opposite where she lived. Contractors arrived one day and proceeded to place 'acrow' props all around the ground floor of the timber framed house. They jacked it up over a couple of days and then started to cast reinforced concrete walls that were positioned partly below ground level and partly above. Once they were completed they dropped the house back down on top of the new basement. I could not believe it. They had created a new floor in about three to four weeks.

Next diary entry:

EVENTS AND PLACES VISITED	
Date	4th September 1965
Place	New Westminster
Weather	It was sunny

Mam and Dad got up late and had lunch went to Eatons with Mary. I went to Anthony's and painted his front fence green (Irish). Mam and Dad left Mary in town and walked back to Anthony's to pick me up then all three of us walked back to Mary's. Then Mam and Dad sat reading while 1.30pm while I was writing up my diary. I was up 'till 12.0'clock pm.

Next diary entry:

EVENTS AND PLACES VISITED	
Date	5th September 1965
Place	Mary's, New Westminster
Weather	Becoming hot sunny to end of day

Mam and Dad walked me to Mass, they got up at 8.45am and walked two miles to St Peter's. Then they came home in the car. This afternoon I went to Uncle Bill's Bar-BQ, Wayne went and gave me an old Lacrosse stick Tonight I'm staying at Uncle Bill's.

Next diary entry:

EVENTS AND PLACES VISITED	
Date	6th September 1965
Place	Mary's New Westminster
Weather	Very hot and sunny
I got up at 12.0' clock noon today and had my breakfast. I had pancakes and then I heard a tape of a man doing impressions. I heard a stereo record then went to Mary's.	

Next diary entry:

EVENTS AND PLACES VISITED	
Date	7th September 1965
Place	Heather and Anthony 's
Weather	Very hot and sunny
Wendy got me up at 9.30am this morning. Then when we got up and had breakfast we went to the sunken gardens at Queen Elizabeth Park, then we went to the UBC the totem poles. Then we went to Stanley Park and had a picnic and saw the animals. Then we went to Capilano Dam and from there we went to Deep Cove.	

Totempoles. Never thought I'd be trying to get one listed in 2005 in "Salford"!!

If it wasn't bad enough watching the house opposite Mary's having a new basement yet another extraordinary event took place. I heard a low rumbling noise, went outside and saw with much amazement a house on a very large trailer. The house was being moved to a new location on the back of the trailer. I could not believe it. They do very extraordinary things in Canada.

A SURPRISE TRIP TO CANADA FROM SALFORD DOCKS IN 1965

Next diary entry:

EVENTS AND PLACES VISITED	
Date	9th September 1965
Place	Harrison Hot Spring
Weather	Good day
Today we went to Harrison Hot Springs, it really is hot as well. There are two springs both covered but only this year there are two taps running all the time and the water is horrid to taste, it tastes and smells of sulphur.	

A SURPRISE TRIP TO CANADA FROM SALFORD DOCKS IN 1965

Mam took a photograph of me drinking the water when I pulled the most horrific face because of the nasty taste of the water. She said "drink up it's good for you". I still don't believe her.

Next diary entry:

EVENTS AND PLACES VISITED	
Date	10th September 1965
Place	Manning Park
Weather	Very good but misty
We had a wonderful trip today by doing 300 miles from Anthony's to Manning Park and back. We saw about 10 chipmunks and I was about a foot away from one trying to feed it. We also saw a big black bear on a garbage dump and was 15 feet away from it. Manning Park is 58.6 miles long. Mam saw a salmon jump out of the Fraser River and I saw a salmon in it. We saw the great land slide at Hope which came all the way down one mountain down into a valley and filled it 275 feet of mud and rock then it went three quarters of the way up another mountain, then fell back into the valley. The land slide blocked 2 miles of the Hope Princeton Highway and filled Ontram Lake from 100 to 200 feet deep of rock and mountain. The slide was triggered by a minor earth quake, 60 million cubic yards of rock and sea bed, or more than 100 million tons. 6,500 feet high from the original road to where the new road and lookout is today.
On the way home we saw a real forest fire. When we stopped to have a look and take pictures of it we could see how it had moved since we were (while we had been) there. Also on the way home we saw a pheasant, and ran one over, but unfortunately for us stopped too far away from it to pick it up	

A SURPRISE TRIP TO CANADA FROM SALFORD DOCKS IN 1965

While I was staying at our Anthony's I used to read the Hunting and Forest Walk magazines. I had read a true storey about a family of four who were on a camping trip through part of the Rockies. They were walking to a clearing to set up camp when they came upon a bear with her two cubs. This is a very dangerous situation to be faced with. The mother automatically goes into protective mode assuming that the "animals" she has encountered want to harm her family. The described in detail how the human family mother (protecting her 12 month old baby) started to run away. The bear chased her 18 year old son, first swiping him across his back and knocking him over. The 12 year old started to climb a tree, not a good idea when being chased by a tree climbing bear. The bear rushed up and swiped off his calf muscles. The bear then chased the father knocking him over and ripping marks across his back. Very frightening stuff.

There was another story about a Forest Ranger who had stopped to eat his sandwiches in a forest, close to a garbage dump, whilst reading his paper. The car window was open and without a sound a nearby grizzly bear, scrounging for food, swung his paw through the open window (presumably for the sandwich) and ripped the mans ear off.

You can tell by now that I was seriously worried about encountering a wild bear. When my Mam got out of the car to take a closer look and to photograph the bear I became hysterical shouting at her to get back in the car before the bear started to chase her. Typically she just laughed.

Next diary entry:

EVENTS AND PLACES VISITED	
Date	11th September 1965
Place	Anthony's
Weather	Fine but it began to rain.
I got up at 10. o' clock then I went to the drug store, then to Woodward's, then home, then the Safeway Store. Came home and then went to Hospital at 5. o' clock to see Aunty Winnie, then after that we went to the White Spot, then we came home.	

White Spot was a restaurant. I used to like eating out. The staff were always polite, funnily enough especially when they heard our accents.

Next diary entry:

EVENTS AND PLACES VISITED	
Date	12th September 1965 Sunday
Place	Anthony's
Weather	Very good indeed.
First of all we went to Mass at St Peter's and took Mary, Peter, Anthony, Anthony, Angela, Mam, Dad and me in our Anthony's car, then we went to Birch Bay in the USA. When we came back they stopped us and took us in the Customs Office, just to get our passports checked. Then we came home. I am sleeping at Anthony's while Mam and Dad are sleeping at Mary's.	

I remember the first time I went to Birch Bay and White Rock. The first thing I did was what my Mam told me to do to dip and my hand in the Pacific Ocean, just to prove that I had been there.

A SURPRISE TRIP TO CANADA FROM SALFORD DOCKS IN 1965

Next diary entry:

EVENTS AND PLACES VISITED	
Date	13th September 1965
Place	Anthony's and Heather's & Wendy C.
Weather	Started to rain at night.
I got up at 20 to eleven this morning, had my breakfast then Anthony came home for his dinner. I went for some milk then I had dinner and started scraping and painting a chair. Then I came up from the basement and while Heather was talking to a lady I washed up and wiped the pots. At the night time I went for my films with Anthony and Wendy C. When I came home I stayed up 'till 1.0' clock next day watching Kay in "The Inspector General'	

In the basement opposite the bottom of the stairs was a peddle Harmonium. With the basement door open into the kitchen I used to play tunes on it to pass the time away Quite often I would play hymns and I used to particularly annoy Heather, while she was in the kitchen, by playing the Death March. She used to shout at the top of her voice, "Can't you play anything else except that thing?" I think her musical taste was somewhat stunted.

It was about this time that I was taken to a Drive-in burger bar. I was sat in one of the rear seats and when we parked up I was asked to wind the window down so that the waitress could clip a tray on to the outside of the car door. The tray had two legs with rubber feet on that rested on the side of the door. The order was spoken into the handset positioned on a post at the driver side of the car. The waitress then brought the order and placed it on the tray. The meal was paid for and when we had finished the driver told the waitress, over the hand-set, and the trays were removed.

Next diary entry:

EVENTS AND PLACES VISITED	
Date	14th September 1965
Place	Mary's and (pen?)
Weather	Great the sun was shining
Mam and Heather went to get their hair done. Dad and I stayed at Mary's for the day. I played with Stella and Paul. At 3.0' clock Mam, Dad, Heather, Wendy and I went to the BC Penitentiary. We went in and looked at things like (Copper pics, leather work and knitting) all done by the prisoners. I met Pat who had wire round his neck in the riot. Heather took Mam and Dad to Woodward's to walk round. Mam and Dad walked to Mary's. We went home, then went to the Pen for Anthony, then to Mary's to pick up a film or films.	

The reference was to the Riot in 1963 when some prisoners took control of part of the prison. Our Anthony was called in urgently and had to be armed. They even had to call out the Royal Canadian Mounted Police. They set up a Bren-gun in the corridor that led to the area of the prison where the rioting prisoners were gathered. Anthony was stood alongside the Mounties as they lay on the corridor floor and their Sergeant instructed them by saying, 'nobody comes along this corridor. If they do, stop them" Anthony also explained how all the officers wore clip-on-ties so that none of the prisoners could take the opportunity to strangle them during any disturbance.

I remember my Mam listening in England to the reporting of the Riot on the Radio/television. She was very worried about our Anthony's safety. When the riot was under control Anthony phoned to say that he was alright, much to our relief.

A SURPRISE TRIP TO CANADA FROM SALFORD DOCKS IN 1965

When we went into the Penitentiary we were allowed into the Warders Office where one of the prisoners was sweeping up and cleaning the was paper basket. Our Anthony brought some of the leather goods that the prisoner or cons(convicts) as they were referred to, had made. Anthony used to look after them in the woodwork/metalwork shops where they made wooden toys, carved leather goods and hammered copper pictures. This was how they were able to earn some money by selling them to visitors. Years ago Anthony had sent my Mam a hammered picture of a miner walking through the Rockies carrying not only his rucksack by his burrow (donkey) as well. I now own it. Anyway I liked the leather wallet that had the head of a Red Indian carved on the front so I bought it. I still have that as well. The prisoner who had made it was imprisoned for trafficking drugs. The swinging sixties eh? Overall I found the visit very interesting.

Next diary entry:

EVENTS AND PLACES VISITED	
Date	16th September 1965
Place	Stanley Park
Weather	Very hot and sunny
Today Wendy went to play school. Mam and Dad walked to Tony's. When Wendy came back we went to Stanley Park and saw most of the animals and fed them, and Wendy and I fed the birds. I also fed a (black) squirrel out of my hand. We saw Totem poles and canoes then went to Prospect Point and saw the LION'S GATE BRIDGE. On the way home the gears broke on the car. Next day Anthony took it in the Pen for Con's (Convict's) to fix it. Mam and Dad walked home in the dark	

EVENTS AND PLACES VISITED
Date   18th September 1965
Place   Tony's
Weather   Great hot and sunny
Anthony and I painted the porch green (Irish). Mam and Heather and Dad went Down Town, then at night we all went to White Spot for supper and then we went down to see the Mountie Wedding. Then Tony drove us round Columbia Street, then to home and bed. xxxxxxxxxxxxxxxxxxxxxxxxxxxxxxxxxxxxxxxxxxxxxxxxxxxxxx Monday night was a fantabulous, suprecalafragilistic sunset!! "

Next diary entry:

EVENTS AND PLACES VISITED
Date   19th September 1965
Place   Round and about New Westminster
Weather   Great hot and sunny
Tony and I went to Mass then we went to Mary's for Mam and Dad, then in Joe's car went to his sister's (Mary). I played with the children and then went over to Malloy's for supper with Uncle Bill, Auntie Winnie, Pat,. Pat, Kelly, Mam, Dad and I. Tony and Heather came while I was looking at Wayne's trophies and scrap books. He wasn't In so I talked to his sister, Mother and Angela Molloy about fouling antics and other things.

Next diary entry:

A SURPRISE TRIP TO CANADA FROM SALFORD DOCKS IN 1965

EVENTS AND PLACES VISITED	
Date	21st September 1965 Tuesday
Place	Anthony's
Weather	Hot and sunny but cloudy
Heather was at play school as an assistant Mother. I did another coat of paint in the porch then watched TV. Then Wendy and Heather came in, Heather made supper, then to bed.	

This entry reminds me of 'Albert and the Lion' There is a sentence along the lines of *"There was nobody murdered or drownded, in fact nothing exciting at all"*.

Next diary entry:

EVENTS AND PLACES VISITED	
Date	24th September 1965 Friday
Place	Downtown
Weather	Great, hot and sunny
We all went downtown to see about reservations for the train ride back. We had supper downtown at The Green Parrot. Walked round the Hudson Bay, bought a few things then came home. Mam went to Mary's then we went to Julia's (Heather's sister), then went to the Ricci's and met Don, Mr and Mrs Ricci also the dog. We had a ride out in the father's Cadillac and saw Vancouver in from the little mountain, then came home	

Next diary entry:

EVENTS AND PLACES VISITED	
Date	25th September 1965, Saturday
Place	Anthon's
Weather	Great
Today I stayed in bed until 12.0'clock, got up and had breakfast, then out the front lawn then I watched TV. We went shopping at the Safeway Store, came back, had something to eat then to Auntie Winnies. Had supper with Auntie Winnie, Uncle Bill, Heather, Wendy, Vin Riley, Stella Riley and Sally something. I baby sat from 9.0'clock until 12.30, all the time watching TV, then we went to bed.	

When we were taken into the Customs Office they said that my Visa was up that day. This was because when we had been to the United States previously my passport had been checked by someone else. They had put a shorter date on my passport than the other person who had checked my Mam and Dad's passports. The Custom's Officer, my Mam, Dad and Anthony were all very amused by pretending that I would probably have to stay in the United States while they went home.

Next diary entry:

A SURPRISE TRIP TO CANADA FROM SALFORD DOCKS IN 1965

EVENTS AND PLACES VISITED
Date 27th September 1965 Monday
Place Anthony's
Weather Great hot and sunny
Today I weeded Tony's garden, then at night we went to Ed Tarling's. Jim Tarling let me play one of their organs(They love them). It plays Xylophone, harp, drums, kettle drums, cymbals, cello, violin and lots more. In Ed's garage is Canada's biggest organ, it is a great size. The organ in the basement is smaller than the one in the living room (one I played), but it is much louder because the speakers are nearer it is a much better sound for beat music, The Beatles.

Next diary entry:

Joe built his own house on the plot next to the white bungalow that they lived in until the big house was completed. He set it all out himself and constructed the foundations and basement walls. When we were there he was up to the upper ground level and it was the noggins for those floor joists that I was working on. The wood that I drilled the holes in were for the herringbone strengthening noggins that are nailed in the centre of the floor joists. This is so that the joists are supported laterally to stop them misting when they are walked on.

One day I was in the back garden, I think I was supposed to be keeping an eye on Paul who was about 5 or 6 years old. I was either reading or playing with some toy cars when I was suddenly aware that he was very quiet. I looked up and found, to my horror, that he was riding his bike up and down the narrow edge of the joists to the ground floor. The floorboards had not been laid and so there was a drop in between the joists of about 2.5m (8 Feet) on to a hard concrete basement floor. I ran in to Mary and screamed for her to stop him.

Next diary entry:

EVENTS AND PLACES VISITED	
Date	2nd October 1965 Saturday
Place	Anthony's
Weather	Fair, at 9.0'clock
Mary had a baby girl at quarter past twelve, that is she had it on Friday night. I am Rosemary Bernadette's Godfather and Angel Molloy is her Godmother.	

Next diary entry:

EVENTS AND PLACES VISITED	
Date	7th October 1965
Place	Church and Mary's
Weather	Fine
Today's date Is 7 October 1965, after Baptising the baby we went to Mary's and had a toast. When I first saw Mary I did not know it was her, but when we were going next she looked like what I expected.	

This is a rather confusing entry. I'm not sure what I was thinking about, unless Mary had had a particularly difficult birth and was unwell.

PART THE SEVENTH
"HOMEWARD TRAIN JOURNEY"

There are no entries for the train journey back, I think this is because I was a bit sad to be leaving the Rockies and the fantastic holiday that I had had.

I remember the strong feeling of loss when we got to the train. The whole process of the reverse journey, Kicking Horse Pass, Hells Mouth, Medicine Hat, Moose Jaw, Revelstoke, Calgary, Banff. The Rockies viewed from within the valleys between the mountains is awesome. The sheer size and magnitude contrasted against the narrow single track railway line clinging to the side of these huge ice formed mountains. I was feeling more and more upset at leaving them behind. This all culminated on the second day when I woke, walked up to the central dome car and watched the Rockies with snow capped peaks get smaller and smaller in the distance. I went to the end dome car and watched them disappear through the glass window in the rear door, seeing the rail track click, clack, click away.

I felt very depressed. The following day I watched the last sunset over the prairies. All the cowboy songs I had ever heard or sang came to mind. Especially the Burl Ives song "In the big rock candy mountains".

We arrived at the Bird's house again and I remember the cake that Dorothy made for our last meal. "Bon Voyage Martins" she had iced on the top. It was a really good meal but tinged with sadness at the thought that I would possibly not see Canada again.

We were driven to the railway station where we caught a local train that took us to Montreal where we stayed with more of my mother's relatives. It was a very comfortable stay over. The following day we were driven to Toronto and the Customs office prior to boarding the Manchester Merchant.

The reverse trip, though sad, was just as good as on the inward journey across lake Ontario, along the Saint Lawrence Seaway and past the Thousand Islands, by the Straits of Belle Isle and out into the Atlantic.

Next diary entry:

EVENTS AND PLACES VISITED	
Date	25th October 1965, Monday
Place	SS. Manchester Merchant
Weather	Fine
Today Dennis and I started a puzzle. To begin with it it has a picture and it has funny shapes, but we will do it. From 10.30pm 'till 12 00pm I was in the engine room with the Chief Engineer. It is bigger than I thought, pipes all over. When I came out Mam and Dad and Captain were looking for me-(they all) THOUGHT I HAD FALLEN OVERBOARD!!	

Next diary entry:

EVENTS AND PLACES VISITED	
Date	26th October 1965
Place	SS. Merchant
Weather	Fine
Today I finished the puzzle, it is 3 men talking and having something to drink, it is in Tudor times. We are supposed to be having the film show tonight.	

Next diary entry:

EVENTS AND PLACES VISITED	
Date	27th October 1965 Wednesday
Place	SS Manchester Merchant
Weather	Rather rough
It has been the roughest day so far , the waves were coming about 15 to 20 feet high, the ship was rocking and rolling from side to side and going up and down-but we are surviving.	

Next diary entry:

EVENTS AND PLACES VISITED	
Date	28th October 1965 Thursday
Place	SS Manchester Merchant
Weather	Rather rough
Tonight we had a film called Major Dundee, there was a lot of shooting and killing. The Captain said after "Joe you will have to get the mop to mop up the blood". We also had a cartoon called Wigwam Wigwam – I think.	

I remember the table cloth twisting and moving sideways and forward and backwards With each roll and pitch of the ship. It was also difficult to hear the words due to the sliding crockery and utensils in the dining room drawers and cupboards.

Next diary entry:

TALES OF FORTY-SEVEN

EVENTS AND PLACES VISITED	
Date	29th October 1965, Friday
Place	SS Manchester Merchant
Weather	Very very rough indeed
Today I had breakfast then we all went up in the lounge. After afternoon the snack my cup of coffee slipped off the table and broke. Then at supper my Mam and I were talking innocently when my soup came all over me. Lucky for me I had a serviette. I am now in bed in m di and the waves are splashing at my porthole.	

PART THE EIGHT
"HOMEWARD BOUND"

We approached darker and darker weather, spindrift and actual waves crossed the bows. The clouds closed in. The ship was tossed this way and that. We were eventually informed by the captain (who was actually the chief engineer, the Captain had been flown back to England before the ship had left Toronto because of a personal tragedy) that we were on the edge of an anti-cyclone. The weather got worse and worse, we were about 300 miles from the west coast of Ireland.

When I went to bed that night I squashed myself into the small space between my suitcase and the bulkhead. By now I was used to the strong movement of the ship. I had become complacent with the rough and tumble movement of the ship and the noise of the developing storm, I fell to sleep fairly quickly.

I had a funny dream that I was tippling over the horizontal bars that surrounded the vacant plot of land at the rear of 47 Broughton Road, this was at the comer of London Street and

A SURPRISE TRIP TO CANADA FROM SALFORD DOCKS IN 1965

Brook Street. I felt the blood rushing to my head and had a little difficulty breathing.

In the morning I went, at the usual time, for breakfast and was surprised at the look on the faces of the stewards. I was full of life having had a very comfortable sleep.

However, the stewards, the Captain, my Mam and Dad all had bags under their eyes and looked very tired. I was confused and asked why they were so clearly tired. The Captain explained that during the storm the ship had experienced a double wave that had caused the cargo in the hold to shift. This shifting of the cargo had caused the ship to roll over to the port side, as usual, but as another wave came immediately after it caused the ship to stay on its port side before it could swing back to the starboard side. The Captain had to steer the ship so that it was heading into the oncoming storm at right angles so that it could ride the anti-cyclone but we did survive.

My Mam could not understand how I had not felt the power of the storm. She said that she thought she had worn her Rosary Beads out by praying all night!!

PART THE NINTH
"HOME ONCE MORE"

When we were being tugged into Ellesmere Port I remember waiting in the lounge. The radio was on and that was the first time I heard the latest Beatle single, I think it was a 'B' side. It was "We can work it out". I hadn't heard any Beatles songs while I was on holiday so I thought it was a great welcoming home present. It reminded me of when Mary handed me a guitar in the hope that I could play one. I couldn't, but from the moment I heard "We can work it out" I was determined to ask our Pete if he would teach me. Fortunately for me he was only too willing. 'Me and Our Kid" is another story!!

When we landed at Ellesmere Port we had to walk along the Quayside towards the Mini-bus that was to take us back to Salford. I started to walk, as I thought, in a normal way to the bus when suddenly the Captain started to laugh and shouted "Joe-you had better get your land-lubber legs". I then realised that I was walking in a zigzag pattern. My body was still walking on the waves, swaying from right to left as if I was still on board ship with it rolling from side to side and pitching forward and aft on the ocean. However, on land this leads you to walk in the zig-zag pattern. The Captain, Mam and Dad found it very funny.

The mini-bus trip along the East Lancashire Road was very mundane after the most exciting trip of my life to Canada. Oh well.

We arrived back at 47 Broughton Road to smiles all around. I remember our John ask me straight away what it had been like.

I told him!!!!!

TM

Appendix

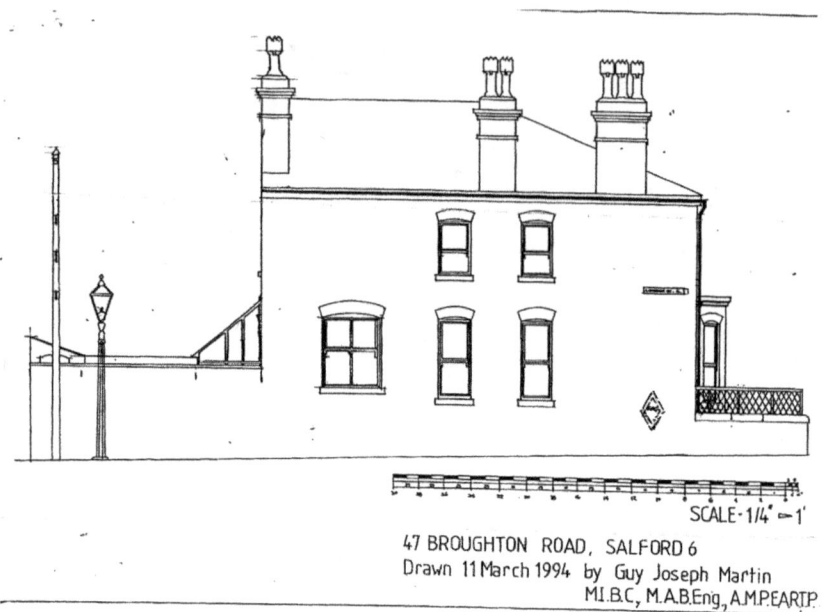

47 BROUGHTON ROAD, SALFORD 6
Drawn 11 March 1994 by Guy Joseph Martin
M.I.B.C., M.A.B.Eng., A.M.P.E.A.R.T.P.

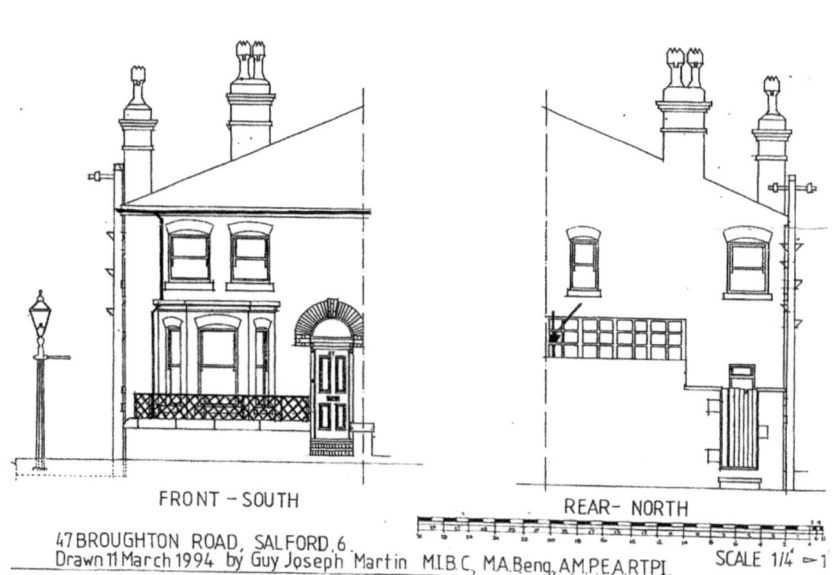

FRONT – SOUTH   REAR – NORTH

47 BROUGHTON ROAD, SALFORD, 6
Drawn 11 March 1994 by Guy Joseph Martin M.I.B.C, M.A.B.eng, A.M.P.E.A.RTPI.

APPENDIX

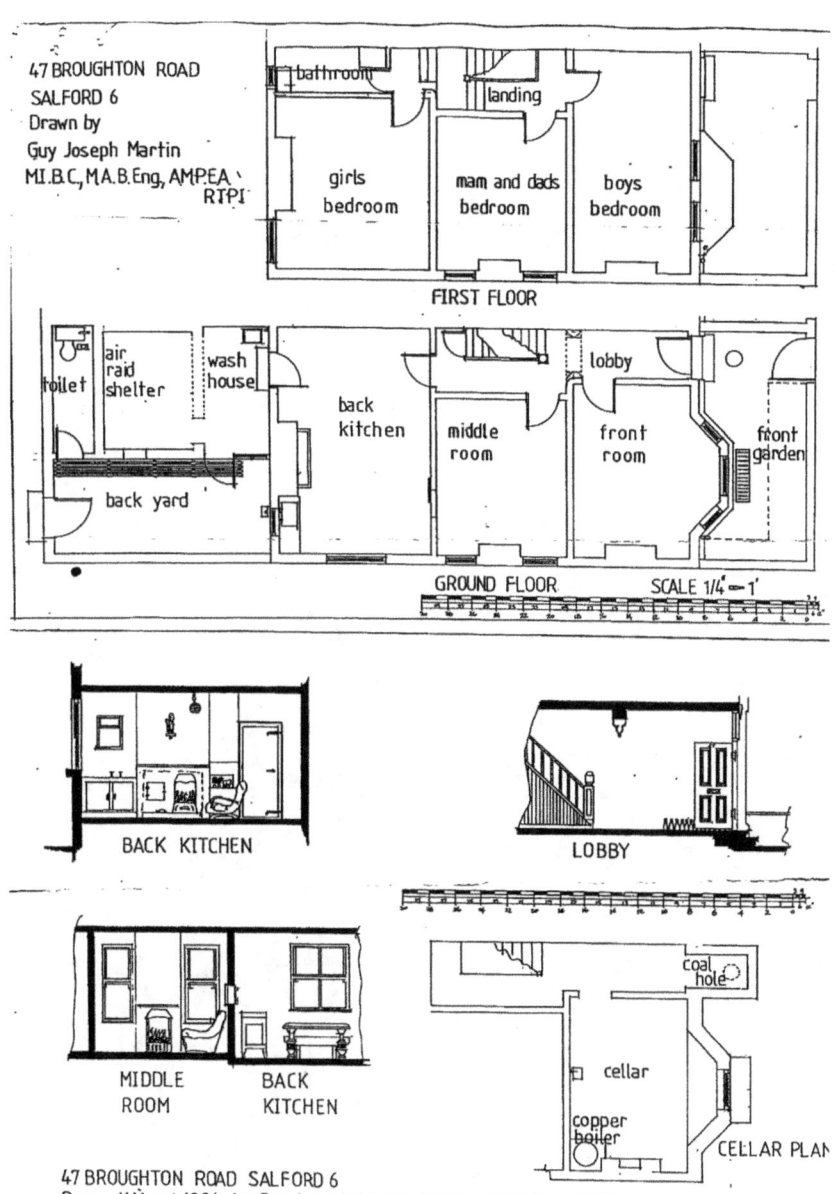

FRIDAY 25th

Mr. and Mrs. Martin
15 Walsall St
Pendleton
Salford 6.
25/3/38.

Dear dadda and mamma

On Thursday 17th a girl had a big thing over her to make her warm. The nurse took it off, and before seven o clock she had died. That girl's bed was next to mine and her name was Dorothy Stockly. I am sending Miss Roney a letter Miss Lauter's Father Corcoran, Rita Robinson, Catherine Priestner, who told me to write back to her.

APPENDIX

> Mary Martin
> C.3.1. ward
> Lodywell.
> 31/3/88
>
> Dear Mamma & Dadda
> Do you know that Weetabix box that you sent me? Well the nurses keep thinking that there is biscuits in the box they say "Who is in that box? Should not you have had them for your breakfast." And I said, "No." and I say what is in. I have sent Miss Lawler a letter. Please send me that story book Rita gave you. Those books are nice and I like the Schoolgirls.
>   Lots of Love
>   From
>   Mary. xxxx xxx x

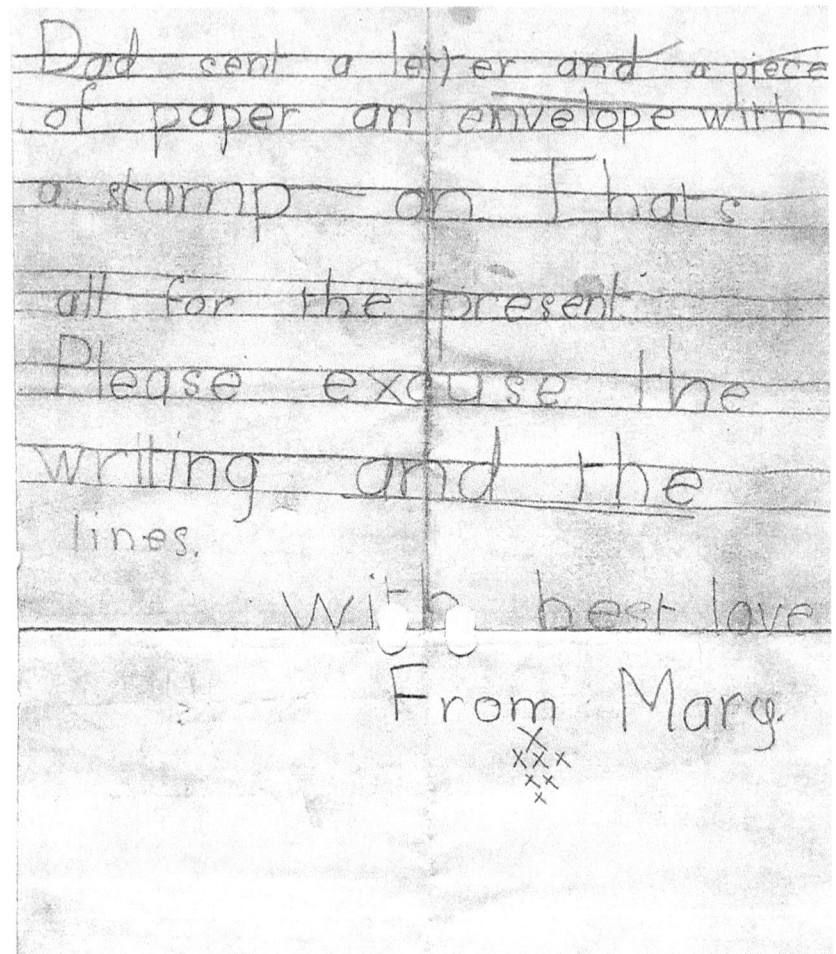

APPENDIX

Dear Mama and Dada,
Nurse Burton said to a girl "Are you Hitler's second child?" She said that because she had her hand up. After she said "He's taught you well". Nearly every day we have a laugh. On Tuesday we were having our usual laugh with doctor Starkey and I laughed so much the tears rolled down my cheeks. Please dont send any crayons. I can't knit just yet sister said. Toodle oo
      Lots of Love
        From
         Mary xxxx xxxx xx

Easter Sund-I
ay
Dear mamma + dadda
Nurse Burton said I will have to wait a little bit longer for cultures because the germ in my nose is not killed. Please send me a pink proggramme of Jack and Jill. Take it out of my desk. I did not get all my Easter Egg the big ward had half and I that half. I am wondering if you could get another proggramme for maureen. Did I send maureen a pink proggramme.
    Lots of Love
        From
          mary

APPENDIX

Easter Monday.

Dear mamma + dadda

I I have some coloured penc[ils]
One is red, one is blue an[d]
one is green. ~~~~~~ my hair [is]
long and straggly and I don't
want sister to cut it but she
said she keeps saying she mu[st]
have to trim it. I think I have
told you I have two pencils. I have
a sharpener, Olivia Olive gave
it to me. We can see Leader Nero
Rd. from here and we see people and
ambulances and motors. We hear the
upstairs singing. We see and hear the
trams. Right outside is Doctor
Edges house and a golfing club,
and we can see them both. We see
all the dead people go to the place
where all dead people go. There is
a greenhouse outside.

little see men upstairs and they wave. Nurse said I am ~~singing~~ growing fatter.

I am — Lots of Love
sending you some ~~paper~~ from
        Mary xxx

Please excuse me but I have lost my pencil and nurse has got the other one. I could hardly write all this in bed. I wrote this letter before doctor came and now I have two pillows. It is my boss Love visiting day Shannon has from every had two pillows mary, six a week and is weeks. or crutches

APPENDIX

> Mary Martin.
> 6.3.1 Ward
> Ladywell Sanat
> Salford 5.
>
> Dear Mamma and Dadda,
> I cannot say much because I won't catch the post. I can have chocolate. There is a big 3.1. and a little 3.1. I'm in the little one and Alan Preston is in the big one. So please tell me what to do about it. Tell Doreen Lomas that there is a sister Dixon, but not nurse Dixon. One nurse calls me Francis and said to me, "Are you IRISH" and I said "no".
>
> Lot's of love
> From
> Mary xxx
> x x
> x
>
> Please let Anthony write
> I wrote Dad a letter on Saturday afternoon

Sunday

Dear mamma & Dadda
I am following Miss Shannon because I got two pillows on monday and she did. She got cutleries on monday and I got them on Sunday 2wth that is today. I put the stamp on upside down. Edmund was right I will be coming soon. I did not know the priest's name because I got no parcel on Friday but I got two on Saturday. I have one envelope and no stamps. I am sending some net home, that I don't want. I dont no wuether I can take my money home, can I send some money home in a letter.
  Love from ×××
      Mary   ×
         ××
          +

APPENDIX

Thursday [~~Wednesday~~]

Mary Martin,
Ladywell,
Eccles,
Salford
28/4/38

Dear mamma and dadda
my cultures are double negative and on Wednesday 27th I was up in a chair. I am expecting to be home for monday. I am up walking. Please give joyce and miss Sanders and maries letters to Rita and tell her to please take them to the right people. I forgot to put miss Sanders letter with maries in the envelope. A girl gave me the envelope ~~with stamps~~ I mean cream one. I have no more stamps and envelopes.

~~Love~~ From
mary xxx
xxx

Ladywell Sana[?]
63-1 ward
Eccles NEW
Salford

My Dear Dadda
and mamma

Today is Sunday and I am a lot better. I had no tea on Wednesday night although I told them I had had no tea. There is a girl in Ward 63-1 and her name is Audrey Thomlinson. I could not write before because I could not get up. Today one [of the] nurse's said to me, "Are you a Cholic?" Yes, I said. So she said, "That's right." The nurse took my oranges off me and gave me on[e]. At teatime, she gave three big Jaffa's like mine away and gave me two slice[s] I don't know wether they were mine or not. When I asked her she said something about "Oh the other kiddies had one each." Dont bother sending any more because I will soon be out. The doctor said My Temparate [is] very good, the nurse said, "Yes". Please do not send any more comics

APPENDIX

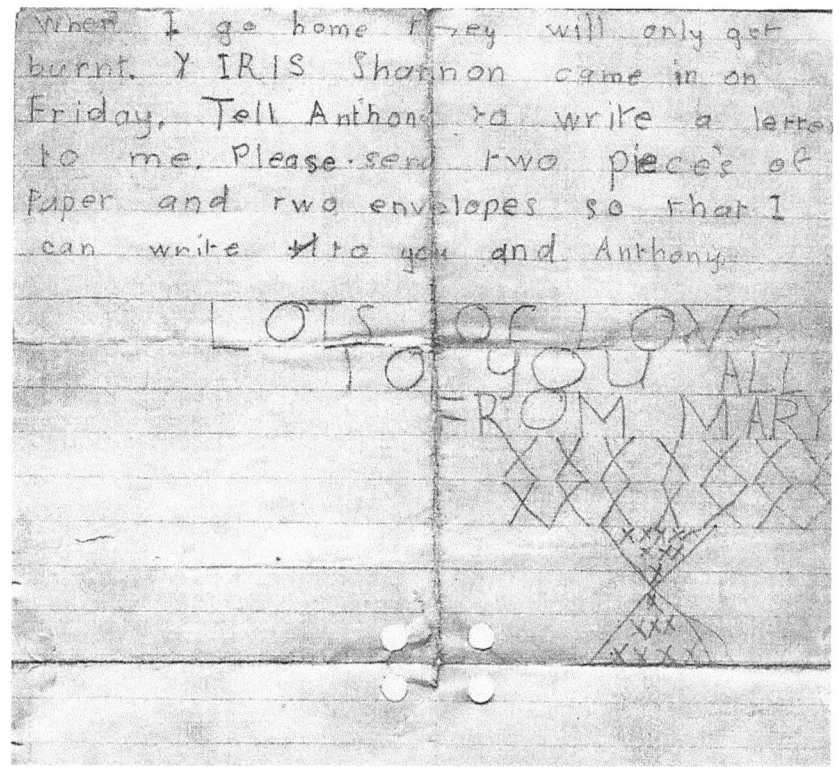

Ladge...
C.3.1. Ward
Salford 5
7/4/38

Dear Mamma + Daddo

Did you send me an exercise book that had nothing in it it's my own. Sister was looking in the cupboard and she found an exercise book with mary in red, Frances in yellow, martin in red. Please ask Edmund to write a letter if he wants to. Alan Preston has the worst nose in bath ward and he was shining a flash lamp on Wedneday night and he got shouted at. It is not bad in here but I want to see you. Please send me a 1d bar of chocolate, all the others get anything they send for.

APPENDIX

Saturday — LADYWELL
Afternoon.   C.3.1 WARD.
                           Salford
                           9/6/3

DEAR GERARD
  WHY Did YOU Not Tell
Me You could not understand
before? I am not scolding you.
Are you still going to school?
Also is Anthony still going?
      I cannot send you
      very long letters like
you send me so Ta-Ta till
another time.
      Love
         from
           Mary xxxx
                 xxx
                 xx

Dear Anthony

I forgot all about you. I could read a bit of your letter. Why don't you write letters like Gerard and I will answer them. Did you get anything off Lily? If so what did you get. Audrey Tomlinson has a net over her cot because she keeps standing up. I can't write any more.

Lots of Love
From
Mary xxxx
xxx
xx
x

am I not a nosey parker

APPENDIX

M. t. M
Ladywell
C. 3. 1. W 9
3 9 18 ord
12/4/3

Dear mamma + dadda
They said it is a 1d and 1½d stamp to Canada it has it in the back. I told Maureen we had a tortoise. Nurse said you are sending me to much sweet things and I have not to have any more chocolate biscuits or sweets only my easter egg if the Rabbit sends it. Well it be alright if sister cuts my hair she keeps saying she will but she might not. Please tell me how many stamps I need to send a letter to maureen. Tell our Joe that if he is saving comics up for the hospital to send all his Goldens because I've only seen one while I am in here. Tell him that now is

his chance to send Golden
Barks and Mickey Mouse
Weekly. He told me he was
saving the comics for the
hospital and I could take them
when I went for a walk with
my dadda.
                Lots of Love
                    From
                       Tapeny xxx

HAPPY
EASTER WHEN IT
COME'S
Please don't send me any toys
or story books only fruit
and comics —

APPENDIX

Saturday afternoon
Ladywell Sanatorium
G.3.I. Ward,
Salford 5
9/4/38.

Dear Mamma + Dadda

I have not had a laugh today doctor Starkey did not come. Another doctor came from his holidays and I don't know what he did. I have a game off Lois Shannon. I am going to pretend that I am a schoolgirl and I have done something wrong and I got a punishment of two hundred lines. The lines are. A stitch in time saves nine. There is only 8 in our ward they are. Renee Andrews, Barbara Bristow, Marjorie Robinson, Doreen Ellis, Lois Shannon, Keith Ralins, and me and somebody else I do not know her name. Audrey Tamlinson went home this afternoon. Keith Rolins is a spoilt boy his dad brings the potatoes. They have a shop. He sees his dad nearly every day, take the potatoes, and he cries. There is a letter for Gerard,

Lots of Love
from
Mary

APPENDIX

I

Ladywell Sanator[ium]
B.3.1. Ward
Solford
8/4/38

Dear mamma & dadda

The buscruits are very nice. One o[f] the other sisters said I am gett[ing] better. Mrs Shannon said their Betty has been in Hope Hospital for 8 weeks and she came in B.1. Ward in Ladywell. She has been in 21 weeks, now (Betty not brin) I wish I could have seen the fire in over back. I cannot do small f'g in real writing. There is a Welsh nurse here called nurse McKernan. We have some nice ~~Daffodils~~ I *mean* ~~have~~ tulips and some white Flowers. Two mistakes? I'm ashamed of myself, I did hardly make one mistake when I was 4. ~~Wubbo~~ / We have to wake up at 4 o'clock every

morning. Mrs Shannon said, "One day their Betty was hiding under the table and her dad was looking for her. She said her dad found her under the table eating the cats fish and enjoying it at that. Mrs Shannon makes us laugh.
            Lots of Love
                  from
             Madamoselle
                 M. F. Martin

Three mistakes altogether.
I forgot to tell you I am writing a letter to Maureen I will not have any more envelopes. Please send me some.

APPENDIX

Ladywell Sanator[ium]
Salford [Ward]
3/4/38

Dear Gerard
I can do a bit of real writing now. Mrs Shannon went to sleep one night and when she woke up again there was a christmas stocking on her locker. Th[at] was while she was in here because I saw it. Every dinnertime I se[e] two or three men their nam[es] are Paddy, George, and Jack. On Saturday it went home it has had Diptheeria and on Saturday it had it's discharge bath, and it went ho[me]. Please tell my mam to send m[y] writing book that she bough[t] for me before I came in her[e] / That ɫ stocking that Mrs Shannon got had a thing in like a pea shooter but it is for blowing bubbles. A boy called Keith said to sister

Iris has one of them things
the doctor tunes you with.
I must say goodbye now

Mistakes.
 and Miss Lots of Love
 Count as From
  Good Many
   Wishes

P.S.
YOU DID NEVILLE GET THIS LETTER
AND PENNY I SENT ON SATURDAY.

Gerard Martin

APPENDIX

smiles, then I smile, and we all burst into a laugh. Do you know that sweet medicine that aunty Margaret had a long time ago I have it now nurse Burson said it will put some colour into my cheeks, the medicine is red. Sister was in the weard and a boy said sister there is a sister matron in the duting room.

Lots of Love
From
Mann

Sunday afternoon
after 2.30.

Mary F. Mrs
Ladybell
Sanata
Saltco

Dear Mama & Dadda
Tell Gerard to write if he wants a letter. I was writing that sentence on Saturday morning but Sister took my pencil and I got it back after the past. I have one pillow and I will tell you when I am on crutches. I am not on crutches yet. You cannot have three pillows but when you get two pillows you are nearly ready for crutches. Please send me some envelopes. A girl out of another ward came in our ward and she has very long plats in her hair. Please do not send any more grapefruit I do not like them much. Nurse Buxton is staff nurse and she told me I would soon be home. We have porridge every morning, and malt every afternoon. Sister always smiles when doctor Starkey comes round she smiles at me and when doctor Starkey

www.ingramcontent.com/pod-product-compliance
Lightning Source LLC
LaVergne TN
LVHW021947060526
838200LV00043B/1946